Walk in the ...... of Jesus —

Ouida Tanner Sides

TO WALK
A COUNTRY
MILE

Wyatt House books may be ordered through booksellers or by contacting:
WYATT HOUSE PUBLISHING
399 Lakeview Dr. W.
Mobile, Alabama 36695
www.wyattpublishing.com
editor@wyattpublishing.com

Because of the dynamic nature of the Internet, any web address or links contained in this book may have changed since publication and may no longer be valid.

Cover and interior design by: Mark Wyatt

All artowrk in this book, including the cover, by Ouida Tanner Sides

ISBN 13 TP: 978-0-9977422-9-9

Printed in the United States of America

Scripture quotations unless otherwise noted are from THE FULL LIFE STUDY BIBLE® NIV® Copyright © 1992 by Life Publishers International, Zondervan Publlishing House. Used by permission. All rights reserved worldwide.

Too Young, lyrics by Sylvia Dee, music by Sid Lippman

Softly, As I Leave You, music and lyrics by Giorgia Calabrese/ Tony DeVita, translated to English by Hal Shaper

The Rainy Day, Henry Wadsworth Longfellow

L'Envoi, Rudyard Kipling

TO WALK
A COUNTRY
MILE

by
Ouida Tanner Sides

Wyatt House Publishing

Mobile, Alanama
www.wyattpublishing.com

"As a personal friend and pastor, my relationship with Ouida Tanner Sides spans over four decades. Reading her account of many events shared together, with added details new to me, was a deeply moving, joyful, encouraging, and faith building experience. I'm sure the Lord will use her story to affect many in the same way, resulting in increased joy and faith in Jesus Christ."

Pastor Mike Barbera (Retired)
Church of the Good Shepherd,
Pass Christian, MS.

"A book that does not invoke pity, but courage."

Frances Coggin Cooper
Tiberius, Israel

"Ouida Tanner's memoirs and testimony is engaging and life changing. As you read her book of life and the Tanners' walk of a country mile, may her contribution bless you as it has hundreds of others."

Tom C. McKenney, Lt. Col, USMC (Ret'd)
*Author, **Jack Hinson's One Man War***

DEDICATION

This book is lovingly dedicated to physically disabled persons everywhere; especially those who are wounded and disabled while serving our country on the battle fronts of the world.

Also, to the care-givers of the disabled, for the dedication and comfort you bring to those you serve. Know that you are a sweet fragrance to the Lord.

Hear the words of Jesus in Matthew 25:39-40: "When did we see you sick or in prison and go to visit you? The King will reply, 'I tell you the truth, whatever you did for one of the least of these brothers of mine, you did for me.'"

I also dedicate this book in memory of my beloved sister, Gwen Powe of Petal, Mississippi, who went to be with Jesus just weeks before this book goes to press. She was a beautiful example of a godly woman and a great influence in my life.

I'll see you in Heaven!

CONTENTS

FOREWORD

Forty-plus years ago, Jim and Ouida Tanner were visiting my family in California. Jim and I were in the back yard relaxing in the late afternoon sun of a beautiful day. I casually asked Jim if he believed there was a Satan, as in the Bible; I didn't. Without the slightest hesitation, he replied, "He's the second-most powerful force in the universe." I was amazed at my own question (I know Who put it my mind), and at his answer. One question—one answer, no discussion. I thought, "If this man, with his brain and his education, believes that, I should re-examine the evidence." This changed my life.

Behind every great man is a great woman. Ouida is that great and godly woman--industrious, tireless, and compassionate. This wife, mother, care-giver, artist, culinary master, and spiritual mentor has spread God's love and hospitality wherever she goes. It has been my privilege to call her my dear friend for over half a century, and I consider it an honor to write this foreword.

I met Jim and Ouida Tanner at Fort Campbell, Kentucky in 1957, four years before his accident. Reading To Walk A Country Mile was a trip down memory lane for me—the bitter and the sweet—and something beyond that. Ouida's memoirs and testimony are told with a humor and charm that will bring enlightenment, inspiration and comfort to your heart.

Tom C. McKenney, Lt. Col, USMC (Ret'd),
author of **Jack Hinson's One Man War**
Marion, Kentucky

INTRODUCTION

As an artist, I have learned that what you leave out of a painting is almost as important as what you put into the work. As in painting, so it is with books. Too many details can obscure the focus. I have memories and stories enough to fill many books. In the case of this book, I pray the reader will be drawn to the light of Jesus as He walked with us throughout our lives. Without His divine intervention in our lives, His saving mercy and grace, His tender love and guidance, I would have no victorious story to share with you.

It is also my prayer that those of you who face difficult challenges in your lives, particularly the disabled, will be encouraged to seek God's help in your struggles.
To the wonderful caregivers, know that you are a sweet smelling fragrance to Jesus. You don't have to go through it alone.

"At the time it happens, I am there." Isaiah48:16
"In all these things we are more than conquerors through Him who loved us….." Romans 8:37.

And now, come along with me as together we *Walk a Country Mile.*

Ouida Tanner Sides

PART I

CHAPTER 1

"THE ACCIDENT"

I had never heard sirens sound so eerie before--wailing as though to announce some terrible tragedy. I felt my stomach tighten as I traced the route the mournful sounds were taking, from the river bridge on the east side of town, following a semi-circle through the main street towards the local hospital.

Later I learned the reason for the unusual shrillness of those sirens. There were several of them, screaming at full blast as the highway patrolman preceded the ambulance in an effort to clear the streets of traffic for this dire emergency.

I had fully expected the telephone to ring as I stood in my front yard talking to two good friends. Becky and Glenn Triplett had stopped by to show us their new car. "It sounds like someone is in need of a doctor," I told them, "And I'm not sure where Jim is."

Jim, my husband was one of two local doctors in the small town of Leakesville, Mississippi. The phone did ring and my heart pounded as I picked up the receiver. The nurse's voice was familiar but the words she spoke to me would forever change the course of my life.

"Mrs. Tanner, Dr. Tanner has just been brought into the hospital. He's been in a wreck."

"Oh, my God! No!" I cried. "Is it bad?" I felt sick. My hands turned cold, my throat felt dry.

"We don't know yet," was her anxious reply.

"I'll be right there." I somehow managed the words.

I stumbled out the door to my waiting friends, fighting for control of my emotions. I began to tremble. It was now five o'clock in the afternoon and a heaviness had been eating at me all day. I had not been able to shake off the foreboding, almost sinister oppression that had plagued me since early morning. I attributed it to the extreme heat of the late May day and the fact that I was two and one half months pregnant with our fourth child.

I readily accepted my friends' offer to drive me to the hospital as well as a neighbor's offer to watch our children. She had just walked across the street to collect her own children who were playing with ours. A coincidence? Hardly!

Word travels fast in a small town. Already a crowd was gathering at the small county hospital. I was ushered into the emergency room where my husband, Jim, was lying on a stretcher.

My first reaction was one of relief. He didn't appear to be too badly injured, or at least there wasn't a whole lot of blood as I had feared. There was a trickle of blood out of his ear and a huge hematoma over his left eye. I remember thinking it kind of strange that he was thrashing his arms about as he moaned and cursed, but his lower extremities were unmoving. I had a fleeting thought that perhaps he had a broken pelvis.

The emergency room staff didn't seem overly concerned about Jim at the moment but were turning their attention to another patient in the room. "This one is hurt really bad." I heard a nurse say as the short-handed staff began emergency procedures.

"Where's Dr. Faulk? See if someone can find Dr. Faulk?" came an anguished cry.

It was a Wednesday afternoon, when the whole town shut down for a midweek afternoon break, even the local doctors. The crowd was swelling; some crying, some praying. Slight comfort.

Someone led me to the doctors' lounge and away from the crowd. A nurse gave me a sedative and told me to lie down on the cot in the room. Voices, some frantic, some whispering, were filtering through to me as the sedative began taking effect. "Dr. Faulk is here......the other fellow just died...."

What did they mean, the other fellow just died? Can't someone do something? What's happening with Jim?

There was a fresh sense of panic among the people in the room with me as a nurse knelt beside the cot, put her arms around me and said. "I'm sorry, Mrs. Tanner, we don't get a pulse or a heartbeat on Dr. Tanner."

My world stopped! The date was May 24, 1961- two days before our tenth wedding anniversary.

"Oh no! no! no! Please God, no! Oh please God.....don't let this happen....please, oh, please God!"

Off the cot, on my knees, with a wrenching cry to the only One who could help in that moment- "Oh, please don't take him, God- Oh, please, Jesus, don't take him, oh, please, please, please....." I could not, I would not, let go of the only life-line that existed. With everything in me, I threw myself on the mercy of God to hear my cry and answer that heart-wrenching prayer. I would not get off my knees. All kinds of thoughts were fleeting through my mind. What if he died? How could we live without him? What would become of our little family? And then the worst thought of all! What would become of Jim if he died? I was not sure of his salvation. That was unbearable!

And finally a voice, I know not whose, "Don't get your hopes up too much, Mrs. Tanner, but we have detected a slight pulse and heartbeat."

HOPE! Oh, thank you, Jesus. There's still a chance- still hope-a small thread to hold on to- a pulse- life-hope!

"We're sending him to a hospital in Mobile. Do you know a doctor there?" My mind wouldn't function. Of course we knew doctors there, but shock was overtaking me and names escaped me.

"Call Jim's parents in Mobile-they'll know." I needed to let my own parents know. I would need help with the children. Oh, my poor children! I needed to go to them. I needed to go to Mobile. I needed to go by our house. Decisions, decisions, somebody help!

The Tripletts would drive me to Mobile, but first by my house and a check on the children. I glanced in my bedroom mirror, what a fright I was in a sundress and no makeup, tear stained face and disheveled hair. No-matter. Grabbing another dress, my purse and little else, I dashed across the street to see our three children; Debby, nine years old; Dawn, who had turned six three days earlier, and Kenny, soon to be four.

I tried to compose myself so as not to unduly alarm the children. I didn't know what they had already heard. The girls were crying as I gathered them in my arms. "Your daddy's been in an accident and we're taking him to a better hospital in Mobile. Mamaw and Papaw are on their way to stay with you all. Try not to worry- I'll be back as soon as I can."

Little arms reached up to me for one more hug as Kenny's three-year old voice said, "Mama, God makes people well".

How many times would I think back on those words in the days, weeks, and even months ahead.

CHAPTER 2
"HOSPITALIZED IN MOBILE"

Nothing in my life had ever prepared me for this kind of trauma. Mine had been a life of relative calm stability- having neither highs of exhilaration or depths of depression. I was basically a happy positive person. Now at the young age of twenty-eight, I was about to enter into a new realm of a life I would never have imagined in my wildest dreams or nightmares.

The sedative was having an effect on me as we arrived at Mobile Infirmary. I was thinking and reacting through a haze. I hardly remember the trip to Mobile.

I heard some bizarre stories about the wild ambulance ride Jim had to the hospital in Mobile. Some say the ambulance made the sixty mile trip in twenty-eight minutes! The young driver later told me, "I just had to get Dr. Tanner to Mobile." He said cars were literally running off the road to clear the way for the ambulance.

From the Leakesville hospital we had managed to make contact with Jim's parents in Mobile who had made arrangements to have doctors standing by when he arrived. One of them, Dr. Lloyd Russell, an orthopedic surgeon, was a very close friend of ours and had attended medical school with Jim.

Dr. Russell began examining him. At this point Jim was semiconscious, " Jim, where are you hurting?" he asked.

"My neck, stupid.!" Jim grimaced.

He had diagnosed his own injury! Except for calling my name, "Ouida....Ouida..." in the emergency room, those would be the last words he would speak for weeks to come.

They would not let me see Jim. There was not a moment to lose when the diagnosis was made: a broken neck! The news was devastating. By now a number of friends from Leakesville had joined us the hospital, as well as my own parents from Waynesboro. When I saw my daddy I fell into his arms and cried, "Oh, Daddy, he has a broken neck." It's one of the few times I saw my daddy cry.

I was living in a nightmare. Jim was in surgery. The solemn faces of the doctors and nurses reflected the seriousness of the situation. All I knew about a broken neck was that the patient either died or was paralyzed for life. I could not bear to think about it.

Dr. Russell said I would not be able to see Jim for several hours and should get some rest. He insisted that I spend the night at his house, which was near the hospital. His wife, Shirley, was also a dear friend and did her best to comfort me. I could have stayed with Jim's parents but they were as badly shaken as I was. Mostly, I wanted to be where I could get frequent updates on Jim. I was unable to sleep, and each time the phone rang my heart almost stopped. A couple of times Lloyd had to go to the hospital. When he came back he would stick his head in the door and tell me Jim was holding his own.

I was unaware that all over the little town of Leakesville and Greene County prayer vigils were being held. I know that I had never prayed so hard in my life, though it was very difficult to concentrate. I was so frightened, so worried, and so very tired. Still I could not sleep. I couldn't remember when I ate last, but I had no appetite.

Thankfully, a lot of memories escape me, but I vividly remember my shock at seeing Jim for the first time. He was lying in a Stryker bed---

an ominous looking contraption with a circular steel frame that almost reached the ceiling. His head was shaved and a pair of metal tongs that looked similar to huge ice tongs were attached to him. The ends of the tongs were cemented into the crown of his head on each side; the other ends were attached to ropes that held heavy metal weights. The function of the weights was to hold the neck and spinal cord taut so the spinal fluid could flow. I was told that the damage to the neck was at the C5 and C6 level.

Tubes were running everywhere. Jim's left eye was swollen shut, large as a baseball and dark blue. His left arm was swollen nearly double and greenish looking. I was told the IV had pulled out of his arm during the wild ambulance ride and the fluid had gone into the soft tissue of the arm. He was unconscious and I nearly fainted at the sight.

The hospital staff would not allow me to spend much time in the room, for obvious reasons. They were constantly attending Jim and the room was crowded with equipment. I spent most of my time in the waiting room on the same floor.

I was realizing the purpose of the strange looking Stryker bed. There were two very narrow mattresses- one of which was suspended above Jim and one on which he rested. He was like a hotdog in a large bun. Every two hours the bed was slowly rotated so that he was either on his stomach or his back. When he was on his stomach, the mattress below him had a hole for his face to fit into, barely two feet from the floor. As the bed was electronically rotated, the weights had to move also. It was necessary for an attendant to hold the weights so that they would not jerk during the motion. Those weights had the important role of straightening out the spinal cord and hopefully the fractured neck bones at the C5 and C6 level.

Thankfully, Jim was unconscious for this would be his home, his position for weeks to come. He would see it all soon enough.

I had many questions for the doctors, and there were many specialists: a neurologist, urologist, cardiologist and our good friend, Dr. Russell, an orthopedist.

"Lloyd," I asked, "How long will he be here?"

He looked at me with such compassion and wanting to let me down gently, replied, "At least six weeks."

"Oh, no! You don't understand. He has to get back to work. We can't afford for him to be off from work that long. You've got to do something."

Lloyd looked at me with tears in his eyes.

"He won't be able to walk for a while."

I felt myself getting nauseated, "What do you mean? How long?"

"You never can tell with paralysis. Sometimes movement comes back fairly quickly , and sometimes it takes a year or longer."

He probably couldn't believe how naïve I was, but he also knew I couldn't handle any more bad news at the moment.

CHAPTER 3
"A NOT SO HAPPY TEN YEAR ANNIVERSARY"

May 26, 1961- 4:30 P.M.- Two days after the accident: Jim's private nurse called me out of the nearby waiting room, "I think you had better go in and see him, or you'll never forgive yourself."

In other words she was telling me it didn't look like Jim was going to make it. He had developed pneumonia, and they had to perform a tracheotomy. It is hard to describe the despair I felt, the helplessness, the loneliness, as I bent over the bed and kissed the forehead of my husband. It was exactly ten years to the very minute that we had exchanged wedding vows. The nurse didn't know that, however she gave me an extra few moments with him.

Ten years! How quickly they had passed. We were married shortly after I graduated from high school. I was eighteen and Jim was twenty. Jim lacked only one summer course to complete his college degree and had already been accepted into the University of Mississippi Medical School in Oxford.

Foolish to marry so young? Perhaps, but we had dated for two years and were crazy in love. We just wanted to be together and it didn't matter that we had no money, no car, no home, only our love-- and to us it was enough. A popular love song that was high on the charts at the time was "Too Young". The words went.... *"They try to tell us we're too young; too young to really be in love. They say that love's a word, a word we've only heard, but can't begin to know the meaning of. And yet, we're not too young to know, our love will last though years may go. And then one day we will recall, we were not too young at all."* It was our song.

Ours had been a small wedding with only my parents, my sister and brother and one of Jim's good friends as best man. I wore the white lace dress my mother had made me for graduation. The pastor of First United Church in Waynesboro, Bro. Ira Sells, officiated. It was my home church and also Jim's when he was in town.

We spent our short honeymoon at the Battle House hotel in Mobile, traveling by bus and train. The hotel was named after a family named Battle, but we were often teased about where we spent our honeymoon. We wanted our marriage to get off to a good start, so we read the Bible together that first night. It wasn't the most romantic setting, a honeymoon on a shoestring, but we had withheld ourselves from sexual relations during our courtship and entered into the covenant of marriage as virgins. They say that ignorance is bliss, and it was through ignorance that I blissfully became pregnant on my honeymoon.

After three brief days together, we returned home where we would live the next few weeks at my parents' home, knowing that we would soon move to Oxford. I had a job at the local bank in Waynesboro and Jim left for Jackson and summer school where he soon graduated from Millsaps College, with a Bachelor of Science degree.

Ten years and three children later, with one in the womb, here we were back in Mobile under very different circumstances. I stood at the window of the hospital watching the raindrops rolling down the glass as my own tears wet my face. The nurse told me it was time to leave. Would I see him alive again? Would the children see their father alive again? They were staying with my parents in Waynesboro and could not have been in better hands. How I longed to comfort them. How I longed to feel their small arms around my neck, comforting me.

CHAPTER 4
"CRISIS UPON CRISIS"

The hospital chapel became my refuge in the days and weeks that followed. It was quiet, comforting, and gave me hope. Our pastor from the Methodist Church in Leakesville visited almost daily. We went to the chapel together and prayed. When the reports were bad, the situation bleak, my spirit at rock bottom, off to the chapel I went. God was there. I could feel Him.

There had probably never been a greater outpouring of love and compassion than we experienced during this time. People came from everywhere to visit; relatives, friends, Jim's patients. Beautiful flowers arrived, only to be left at the nurses' station or the waiting room because Jim's room was crowded with equipment. Most of the time I sat in the waiting room down the hall and that is where I slept, when I slept. Despite my utter weariness, I found sleeping difficult. My stomach growled from hunger, yet food seemed to stick in my throat.

One night when my parents and sister were visiting, Dr. Russell told them to take me to a nice restaurant and order me a steak and a glass of wine. Wine? I had never had a glass of wine in my life. How could I do that? Drink wine while my poor husband lay dying? Still it was doctor's orders and my folks intended to carry them out. A few sips of the red vino went straight to my head, especially on an empty stomach. I immediately got a little dizzy followed by a guilt trip and a crying jag. But the steak stayed down and made me feel better.

Gradually Jim's condition improved, not without constant complications, however. The veins in his arms collapsed, and the doctors had to do cut-downs on the veins in his legs. Since he was still in a coma, he was tube fed. His bouts with pneumonia and the tracheotomy that had been performed required frequent suctioning of his throat. He suffered phlebitis in his legs and also had kidney infections.

I was allowed to stay in the room more often. I sat or slept in a chair in a corner of the crowded room. I had begun to feel deep depression. Added to this was the fact that I was spotting and feared losing the baby I was carrying. At that point I was about three and a half months pregnant.

Because of Jim's critical condition, his parents and I felt that a family member should always stay overnight at the hospital. Hospitals were different in 1961. The hospital staff broke some rules by allowing one of us to sleep on a cot in a nurses conference room across the hall. It was better than sleeping in the waiting room but there were frequent interruptions. Jim's mother was a great help but his father had resorted to his old habit of drowning his sorrows in alcohol.

Slowly Jim began to wake up from his unconscious state. He often groaned and began to move his arms a little. I became quite concerned when I saw him lift his shoulder slightly upward while he was on his stomach. I was worried that he might push his body upward and flip off the narrow bed and expressed my concern to the doctor. Orders were given that Jim be strapped to the bed when on his stomach on the Stryker. And then one night it happened! The night nurse had not put the restrainer straps on and Jim flipped right off the bed, jerking the tongs out of his head.

Across the hall, Jim's mother was having a bad dream. She dreamed that Jim fell out of the bed and pulled the tongs out of his head. She awoke to find her dream had become a reality.

Instead of being taken to surgery, the tongs were reinserted into Jim's head then and there.. This would prove to be a major problem later, due to infection.

Jim later said that the fall out of bed was his first recollection of anything since the accident. Daily he became more conscious, but it brought with it a new set of problems. He became more agitated, obviously suffering from pain and confusion. His mind was not yet clear so he did not understand what was happening to him; especially he did not understand the rotation of the Stryker bed every two hours.

Each time the bed passed the zenith position and began the face downward turn, he was terrified. He had the awful feeling of falling, and would cry out, "Help, somebody, don't let me fall!"

It was reassuring if a family member stood by him, touching him, soothing his fears. We tried to have someone there every two hours when he was turned, which meant whoever was sleeping across the hall had to be awakened.

Crisis upon crisis, the days dragged on. We had to hire private duty nurses around the clock because of Jim's critical condition. They had to be paid weekly. I had other financial woes, too, as I knew our bills were accumulating back home. To complicate matters, my obstetrician had ordered me to bed. My spotting had increased and he was concerned for me. Now what was I to do? Jim's mother and dad had to work. I needed to stay at the hospital. I was worried about our children and I was worried about my parents. They had been taking care of the children since the accident but also had another family crisis to deal with. My brother's wife, in Louisiana, was having difficulty with her first pregnancy and almost died of uremic poisoning and high blood pressure. My parents needed a break from the children, so I arranged for someone to bring them to Mobile where I kept them at Jim's parents' home and tried to rest in bed.

My poor children; my heart went out to them. I tried to shield them from as much of the bad as I could. They were allowed to see their dad for the first time once he regained consciousness. I was concerned how they might react at his appearance. Jim had lost almost half of his body weight and looked so bad. I didn't want the children to see the tongs sticking out of his head, so we draped towels around his head. He managed a weak smile for them while we held them up to kiss his face.

It was impossible for me to spend all my time resting in bed. The

28

spotting gradually improved and I was able to make a trip to our home in Leakesville to take care of business matters and get fresh clothes. I was rarely gone for more than a few hours. I had begun to wear maternity clothes earlier in the summer but now seemed to be losing weight and no longer needed them.

I was constantly bombarded with financial woes. I had retained Jim's office nurse at his clinic in Leakesville who kept the office open for a few hours a day. Some of his patients came in for routine injections and blood-pressure checks. Some paid a little on their outstanding accounts. If only they had paid in full we could have been solvent for a while. To add to it all, we had no health insurance.

It was a rainy summer. I stood at the hospital window and wished for the sun---anything to brighten my spirits. Friends visited, and there were dozens of beautiful get-well cards, many with scripture verses in them. One scripture that was quoted more often than all others was Romans 8:28. "For we know that God causes all things to work together for good to those who love Him and are called according to His purpose."

For the life of me, I didn't see how anything good could come from such a tragic accident. Jim was needed as a doctor in the rural community of Leakesville and the Lord knew how much the children and I needed him. It would be years before I could reconcile that scripture to our situation.

And so the summer dragged on. My mind was completely overwhelmed with all our problems: Jim's health, the children, our finances, our future and my own health. I slept more and more in the chair in Jim's room to try to escape reality. Jim was now alert enough to face reality, and his own depression was eating away at him. Visitors often had to sit on the floor and look at his face in the hole in the mattress and try to converse with him. One such visitor was his old friend, Dr. Howard Thomas of medical school days. He was one of several of Jim's friends that I had written to and informed of his accident.

Any improvement in Jim's condition was quickly diminished by setbacks. By this time he had developed osteomyelitis of the skull bone, a type of staph infection. The tongs had to be removed, the holes in his skull surgically repaired, and a tortuous neck brace put into place. The Stryker bed was removed from the room and things seemed a little more normal on the surface. However, depression was weighing heavily on him. As a medical doctor, he knew only too well the prognosis of his case. He was getting some return of the movement in his arms and hands, but he still could not feed himself or even brush his teeth. It was easy to see his will to live was waning.

I tried so hard to be optimistic around him, assuring him that things would soon be back to normal---we would lick this thing. He had no appetite and of course it was hard to move his jaws with the tortuous neck brace. The hospital dieticians did their best to prepare appetizing food but nothing helped. Finally, we brought in some of his favorite fast foods, milkshakes and steer-burgers from a local restaurant which proved to whet his appetite. One beautiful sunny day the nurse took him outside in a wheelchair hoping the fresh air and sunshine would refresh him. Visitors who were coming to visit him passed him by, not recognizing him. He only weighed ninety pounds at thirty years old.

I did not know it at the time but Jim was having a recurring dream. He did not share it until years later, but in the dream he was standing on the caboose car of a train and preaching the gospel to people during whistle stops. It was somewhat prophetic in that God would use him in years to come to promote the gospel.

CHAPTER 5
"OUR EARLY YEARS TOGETHER"

Ineeded to be in several places at once, but I felt I was needed at the hospital most of all. There I sat, day after day, with so much time on my hands, and too much time to think and worry. I reminisced a lot. My parents, Leslie Hall Trigg and Mittie Freeman were married over fifty-seven years and lived most of their lives in the small town of Waynesboro, Mississippi. Mama was Baptist and Daddy was Methodist. While we visited both churches, we eventually settled on the Methodist.

Our home was a modest two bedroom wood frame house with a tin roof. There's nothing like rain falling on a tin roof to put you to sleep – or wake you up! Fireplaces were our sole source of heat except for Mama's big old cast iron stove. She was the best cook in the world. From her I learned the gift of hospitality because guests were always welcome. She was an excellent seamstress and often earned extra money as such. She also had a reputation for her green thumb, growing beautiful plants and flowers. She was the affectionate parent, always giving us children lots of hugs and pulling us into her lap, even after we were grown.

Daddy was quiet, steadfast; a man of his word. His handshake was good as gold. He was an electrician and a hardware and furniture salesman, but never had a high-paying job. He was a good money manager though and we never lacked the basic necessities. He had a small farm and raised Hereford cows, hogs, and chickens, as well as huge gardens of vegetables. Most of our food was organic before it was in vogue. He was very generous with his gardening and provided fruits and vegetables for many of our relatives and lots of neighbors.

I was the middle child of three. Born at home in 1932, I almost didn't survive birth at only two and a half pounds. My first cradle was a shoebox. I always looked up to my older sister, Gwen because she was such a good and kind person. She had blondish naturally curly hair while mine was dark and poker straight. I learned to appreciate classical music by listening to her practice piano.

My brother, L.H., was two years younger. We played marbles and with toys fashioned out of thread spools and rubber bands. We had our share of quarrels and sometimes got into trouble, but survived our childhood. He became an electrician like Daddy.

Growing up I loved anything to do with art—coloring books and crayons, watercolors, modeling clay, paper dolls. Sometimes I drew my own paper dolls and cut some out of the Sears Roebuck catalog. One of my favorite things was collecting small clear bottles with interesting shapes, filling them with colored water and setting them on the window ledge in my bedroom. There were no art classes at Waynesboro High School, but I had an elderly science teacher who was also an artist and recognized my ability. She offered to teach me to paint with oils after school at no cost. She even provided the materials free. I will always be indebted to Ms. Beulah Delano for setting me on the path to become an artist.

Jim Tanner was born on December 23, 1930 in Reform, Alabama, a very small town near the Mississippi town of Columbus. He was the second son of Kenneth and Gretchen Tanner. His brother Bill, was eighteen months older than he. The family moved a lot due to Mr. Tanner's job as a furniture salesman. They had lived in North Carolina near the furniture factories; also in Memphis, Tennessee and finally settled in Mobile, Alabama. His father served in the Navy during World-War II and his mother worked at Brookley Air Force Base where she inventoried airplane parts.

Jim and Bill were pretty much on their own as teenagers but were close as brothers and were avid baseball fans. Jim delivered newspapers and used his money to support his hobby of collecting stamps.

Bill and Jim graduated from Murphy High School in Mobile at the same time. Afterwards, Bill joined the Navy and Jim entered Spring Hill College.

It was at this time that Jim came into my life. I knew who he was because his grandparents owned a boarding house in Waynesboro and Jim often visited there in the summers. He was rather a scrawny kid, but it was a well-known fact that he was considered a genius because of his extremely high IQ. I used to see him riding horseback around town but had no interest in him. His grandparents sang in the choir at the Methodist Church, and it was at the youth meetings at that church that I first got to know Jim personally. He asked me for dates a couple of times, but I had no interest whatsoever in dating him. As a matter of fact, I detested him. He was a prankster and was always pulling tricks on people, like throwing a bag of water in the mayor's face one Halloween night. There were rumors that Jim and some of his friends went nude streaking across the downtown store roofs.

Once, his friends took him to the local cemetery and tied him to a tree with ropes and left him there. When they got back to the downtown area a mile away, there was Jim sitting on a street curb panting like a dog! My personal peeve with him was that he had tossed firecrackers at a cousin visiting from Illinois and me one New Year's Eve. I heard him say "Let's get the Yankee!"

I couldn't believe it when my best friend, Joyce, started dating him. "He's really not so bad, in fact, he's pretty nice." she told me. Well, she could have him, I had my eyes on somebody else.

And then one afternoon as I was on my way to church for a youth hayride, our paths crossed forever. "Where are you going?" he wanted to know. He started walking with me.

"To a hayride, are you not going?"

He was dressed in blue jeans, a sweaty white tee-shirt and cowboy boots. "Naw, I'm tired. I've been working with my uncle all day doing construction."

That's good, I thought as we were walking along the street in front of his grandmother's boarding house. His mother, grandmother and great-aunt were sitting in rocking chairs on the front porch of the grand old house. Without warning, Jim grabbed one of my arms and twisted it behind my back saying "Ask my mother if I can go with you to the hayride."

"I WILL NOT!" I retorted furiously. The twist tightened; he was hurting me.

Through clinched teeth I asked, "Mrs. Tanner, is it alright if Jim goes with me to the hayride?"

She played along with his ridiculous request, "Don't you think he's a little young?" I'm sure I turned beet red, both from embarrassment and anger.

I couldn't shake him from my side on the hayride. Furthermore, my own boyfriend was with someone else, adding to my misery. When it was over there was no-one to walk me home except Jim and I sure didn't want to walk alone in the dark. At the door Jim asked to take me to church on Sunday night. I declined, but he was there anyway, and from that time on until he returned to college a few weeks later, we saw a lot of each other. Joyce was right. He wasn't so bad once you got to know him, and he was interesting to talk to, very learned on a great variety of subjects. We agreed to write to each other.

Jim was a junior in college and I was a junior in high school, although there were only two years difference in our ages. He was brilliant. He lived eighty miles away but came to visit his grandmother as often as possible, in order to see me. We wrote each other almost daily, and it was clear that we were falling in love.

Perchance, exactly one year from that first hayride, we went on another church hayride; this time to Lake Waulkaway forty miles away. It was a summer camp retreat area with Olympic size pools and pavilions. Ever the pranksters, Jim and his friends decided to pull a joke on the crowds there. One of the guys got on the loud speaker and announced that a famous female diver from Brazil was going to perform a high dive. People came running from the pavilions and their picnics. The spotlight was on and "Miss Carmella " took her place on the sixty foot diving board. This celebrity was none other than Jim Tanner dressed in a one-piece yellow satin swimsuit with matching swim cap, hairy legs and all. He really had planned to do a fancy dive, but when he looked down from that lofty height, he got a little nauseated and did a leaning walk off the board with a mighty splash. In unison the disappointed crowd sighed "Ohhhhhhh……"

"Who is that?" someone asked me.

"I have no idea." I fibbed, too embarrassed to admit I knew him. It wasn't funny at the time- but it was part of the personality of Jim Tanner.

He had a serious side of course and he had a goal for his life, which I liked. Most of boys that I knew didn't have the foggiest idea of what they wanted to do with their lives, but Jim had plans to go to medical school. I had often said I would never marry a doctor because of their busy lives and dealing with so much sickness, but I began to change my mind.

I had plans of my own for my future before Jim came along. I loved art and wanted to attend art school, especially since the lady who taught me art had high aspirations for me. My parents were supportive of my art activities but never seriously sat down and discussed an art education for me, else I might have taken a different route. Nevertheless, Jim and I were married soon after I graduated from high school .

We were so happy that first year of our marriage. Even the fact that I got pregnant on our honeymoon didn't discourage us. We had talked about wanting children before we were married, but naturally didn't expect this to occur so early on. We decided that it must be God's will and didn't question it. Jim graduated from Millsaps College with a Bachelor of Science degree and began medical school shortly thereafter.

He found student housing for us in converted army barracks on campus at Ole Miss. A two-bedroom apartment rented for $12.50 a month. There was a small living-dining room and a very tiny kitchen, two bedrooms and a bath. The walls were so thin you could hear the clock ticking in the next apartment. We had a kerosene stove, an ice-box (yes, ice box, not refrigerator) and a double sink, no cabinets. The ice-man delivered ice two or three times a week at a cost of fifteen cents per block. Most of the time it had melted before the next delivery. We had to buy milk and meat almost daily because it would easily spoil. We had no car, so we walked the distance to the small grocery store.

In fact, we walked almost everywhere we went. Our only source of entertainment was to walk to the Student Union Center on Saturday nights to watch the only television set that we knew anything about. Television was just hitting the markets and of course terribly expensive to own. Our furniture was early attic-hand-me-downs from relatives. We had received some lovely wedding gifts of china, crystal, silver, etc. but they were not ex-actly practical. Never-the-less, I set about to make our first home as pretty and cozy as possible. Our total income was $122.22 a month, provided by the State of Mississippi as part of Jim's scholarship to medical school. We had not expected things to be so tough when we got married. We had as-sumed that I would be working while Jim was in school. We were too glad to be together to realize how bad off we were.

Soon after I had joined Jim at Ole Miss, I was busying myself with unpacking. He had not indicated to me what the boxes held, and I had the fright of my life when I opened a box full of human bones including a skull! Jim, with incredible sense of humor, thought it was hilarious.

Weeks later, Jim got the boxes of bones out and spread them on the living room floor. He was studying anatomy and had to learn each bone and where it connected to the proper bone. Like the song, "Oh, the hip bone connected to the leg bone, and the leg bone connected to the knee .." Jim proceeded to assemble this skeleton in the middle of the living room floor with orders for me not to disturb it until he could show his fellow classmates. He often tutored other medical students in our apartment.

It was time for our scheduled delivery of ice and our ice-man was a black fellow in his forties. He had to step over this sprawled out skeleton to get to the icebox. His eyes bulged at the sight, the ice tongs began to tremble in his hands as he hastily deposited the block of ice forgetting the fifteen cents I had left for him.

We had no washing machine, no car or money to go to the laundry mat, so I did the laundry by hand in the double sink. It was very difficult to wring sheets and towels by hand. Our first Christmas present to each other was a $10 washing machine, small enough to fit in the kitchen sink, but it had an electric agitator. It would only hold one sheet at a time or a couple of towels. A hand-operated wringer was attached to one side. It was better than washing by hand, but just barely.

Our baby was due in late February. We had fixed up the extra bedroom as a nursery. I hand painted a border of animals around the wall in watercolor. We had been given lots of baby clothes, which I washed and ironed and could hardly wait to use. Our first purchase of furniture was a baby-bed from the Sears Roebuck catalogue. We were hard pressed to stretch our small paycheck from month to month, but we were happy.

Two weeks before our baby was to be born, I went to be with my parents in Waynesboro. It was better for all concerned for me to be there, so that my mother could take care of me. Luckily, my due date of February 24 fell on a weekend. Jim was able to make the 250 mile trip from Oxford. I was already in labor when he got there and he was quite nervous. In fact, he was so nervous the night she was born that he forgot to eat supper at his grandmother's boarding house. Apparently hungry, he went across the street to a movie theatre and bought popcorn and an ice cream cone. Between labor pains I asked what he was eating. "Oh, I brought this to you." was his nervous reply. That was my Jim!

Deborah Ethel (after Jim's grandmother, Ethel) arrived at 11.30 PM on February 23, l952, weighing in at 6 lbs. 6 oz. She was a little doll, with a head full of black hair. Jim was allowed in the delivery room since he was a medical student, and his own child was the first birth he had witnessed. What a thrill! It was too bad he had to leave the next day to go back to school.

Our income tax refund arrived just in time to pay for the medical expenses, although the doctor did not charge for the delivery. With that extra blessing I encouraged Jim to buy himself a new pair of pants and a shirt as his wardrobe was pitiful. When I next saw him I could hardly believe what he had selected! Chartreuse pants, a yellow shirt, and a black and chartreuse checked, pleated tie! I was mortified! He would have to wear these a long time. He said one of his professors told him, "Tanner, you look like a grasshopper." I got so tired of washing and pressing those bright clothes for what seemed like years.

Chapter 6

"Remembering the Day"

Jim had now been in Mobile Infirmary for about ten weeks. It seemed much longer, like an unending nightmare. He was slowly improving despite setbacks such as bladder infections and bedsores. His depression made him a bitter patient and he became uncooperative. I didn't know how to cope with his depression, especially since I was battling my own. I read him the many cards and letters that came from near and far. Ministers visited and prayed with him. He wasn't very responsive.

I had managed to go to Leakesville in June for our son Kenny's fourth birthday, but for the most part the children were still with my parents or my sister. It made me nervous to drive the distance to Leakesville, especially since the route took me very near the road where the accident happened. I never went to see the spot, and never wanted to see the car. The thought was too unnerving. I had, however, been able to piece together more details about the accident. It had happened on a curve on a rural road between the Alabama state line near Citronelle and Highway 63 in Greene County, Mississippi near Leakesville.

Jim was a passenger in a car owned and operated by Floyd Sullivan, a military jet pilot who was home on leave and who Jim had only met the day before. I, myself, had met Floyd briefly early the morning of the accident at the home of a mutual friend, Martin Platt. Martin was a quadriplegic, the result of polio years before. Jim was both a good friend and personal physician to Martin and often dropped by to see him. Martin and his wife had planned a fishing trip that day and invited me along. It wasn't the kind of thing I liked and could not understand why I had agreed to go with them, but for some reason I did.

Jim just happened to drop by the Platt's house that morning of May 24. Floyd had also dropped by their house hoping to get Martin to run some errands with him in his brand new white Buick. Since Martin had already made plans, Jim volunteered to ride with Floyd after he saw a few patients at the clinic. Something deep in my spirit reacted strongly to that idea. Across the room I looked at Jim and shook my head "no", but to no avail.

The entire time that we fished that hot, humid day, I had a gnawing feeling that something was wrong. I couldn't put my finger on it- had nothing to base anything on, but I couldn't shake the feeling. When I got home about mid-afternoon, I told our maid, Paralee who had been watching the children, that I felt very weak and strange. She suggested that I lay down and rest. She also told me that Jim had called about 1:00 P.M. to ask if his dad had come from Mobile. He had planned to visit Jim that afternoon. He never came however.

Jim and Floyd had ended up going to Citronelle, Alabama to look at baseball lighting equipment. The accident happened on the return trip home, about seven miles out of town. It was a one-car accident. The car was traveling at a high rate of speed, ran off the road and overturned several times, landing upside down. It happened in front of a country church where two preachers standing outside were the first to reach the scene.

It was in the days before seat belts were standard equipment in automobiles. According to witnesses, Floyd was able to drag himself through a window and collapsed on the grass. Jim was trapped inside, already turning blue. Somehow, they got him out. A lady who lived in a nearby house was holding Jim's head in her lap as someone pulled his wallet out of his pocket for identification. "Oh, my God!" she screamed, "It's my doctor!"

Jim was apparently unrecognizable.

Moments later I heard the awful sirens and knew they were the reason for the foreboding feelings I had been experiencing all day. I am fully convinced that our spirits know things long before our minds do.

One thing that I will be eternally grateful for is the fact that Jim and I had been getting along very well together, no serious arguments or ill feelings toward each other. At least in that respect, I had no regrets.

Many years later, as I recall this event, I often wonder how different things might have been had Jim's father come to visit that day. He dwelt on that fact himself as guilt consumed him for not going to Leakesville as planned.

I have also wondered why I had accepted Martin's invitation to go fishing with him and his wife that day. Jim was the fisherman, not I. Had I not been there at that exact time of day, I would have missed the opportunity to meet Floyd Sullivan. I would not have known what Jim was doing during the remainder of the day. All I knew was that I did not enjoy the fishing excursion, nor could I account for the strange foreboding in my spirit.

Why did the accident happened in front of a country church? Why were two preachers the first to reach the scene? Years later I would read in Isaiah 48:16, "At the time it happens, I am there." Taken out of context you might say. Maybe, but it brings me comfort. God is in control.

CHAPTER 7

"OUR FRIENDS THE THOMASES"

One way that I employed my waiting time in the hospital was to inform friends of Jim's accident and our present state. Many of those friends responded by sending letters and cards, and a few came from hundreds of miles to visit. Among them were two of our dearest friends from medical school and internship days Dr. Howard and Ann Thomas.

We were friends when the guys were fellow students at the University of Tennessee Medical School in Memphis. We became like family when both families moved to Atlanta to do a year's internship at St. Joseph's Infirmary. We lived across the street from each other in a low-rent housing development and the men had the same work hours at the hospital in order for Jim to ride with Howard. We still had no car at that time.

The Thomases had two sons, Jimmy and Bobby. We had our daughter, Debby and our second daughter, Dawn Suzanne, was born in May of that year--1955. She was the spitting image of her older sister at birth, except she perhaps had even more hair. In fact, she was the talk of the hospital because the nurses liked to put ribbons in her unusually long and thick black hair.

The two families were inseparable. A local Methodist church had a mission out-reach church in one of the apartments in the development where we lived and we sometimes went to services there. Both families were living on very limited budgets and about our only recreation was visiting with other interns and their wives. Occasionally we were invited into the homes of local doctors for dinner and it was at these affairs that Ann and I were introduced to cocktails and fine dining such as we had never known, both being small town girls. We felt terribly out of place, but also wanted to "fit in" this new society.

During the hot summer of that year, while the men were working at the hospital, Ann had the frightening experience of a prowler trying to break into her apartment. It was not a good neighborhood, so we set about finding a better place to live. We found a house that had been divided into two apartments, while sharing a common living room. It would work great for us. We drew straws to see who got upstairs and who got downstairs. The Tanners drew the downstairs. The arrangement worked very well and the two families grew even closer as friends. When the internship ended, we tearfully went our separate ways, not realizing how drastically our lives would change in the years ahead.

The Thomases moved back to Tennessee where Howard set up a medical practice, and Jim was drafted into the army. Our paths would not meet again until four years later and under drastic circumstances. Jim was in his first year of his own general medical practice when he was contacted by Howard Thomas' father and asked if he could come to Tennessee to see if he could help Howard and Ann. They had become addicted to drugs and their lives were falling apart.

The demands of a small town doctor had been too much for Howard. The irregular hours, lack of sleep and general pressures had caused him to succumb to taking sleeping pills to sleep and amphetamines to wake him up, resulting in a vicious cycle of stronger and stronger drugs. They were also caught up in a social life that neither were accustomed to. Ann found herself involved in a lifestyle of partying, drinking and eventually joining Howard in using drugs.

We were stunned at the news. This couldn't be happening to our dearest friends. They were wonderful people, family oriented, church goers.

I had never known anyone with drug addiction and couldn't conceive of such devastating results. Jim and I made arrangements for someone to care for our children and traveled to Tennessee to see what we could do, if anything.

We were in shock when we saw them. I had always considered Ann to be one of the most beautiful women I had ever seen, raven black hair, hazel eyes, olive skin and a knock-out figure. She had modeled clothes for some fine stores in Memphis during our medical school days. Now, she was a mere shadow of that person, probably weighing less than eighty pounds, eyes glazed over, disheveled hair, and her lovely skin now pocked with sores. Her arms and legs showed evidence of needle marks. It made me sick to my stomach to see her in that condition.

Howard didn't look any better. Once a handsome, tall, stately looking man, he was unkempt, glassy-eyed, dirty and his shoulders drooped at a peculiar angle. They hardly acknowledged our presence, but retreated to the bathroom where they continued shooting up drugs and picking at sores on their bodies, which they thought were full of parasites and worms.

Their precious young sons, which now numbered three, were being cared for by a wonderful black lady, nicknamed "Cat" for Catherine. She must have been an angel because she loved the family so much and did her best to take care of them.

Try as we did to help them, our efforts were useless. We left feeling utterly discouraged and shaken. We felt so sorry for Howard's parents and wished we could have had some positive influence on Ann and Howard.

And now, another year later, these same friends had driven 500 miles to see Jim in Mobile Infirmary. They both seemed to be better and had their children with them. Jim was on his stomach on the Stryker frame when Howard came in to see him. Howard had to sit on the floor and lower his head to be able to look into Jim's face. It was heart-wrenching for both of them—they were such good friends. The visit was brief and later I found out that Howard was so devastated at Jim's condition, he drove like a maniac on the way back to Tennessee, nearly killing his family. He sank deeper than ever into his drug addiction.

God had not forsaken the Thomases or the Tanners, however. Their lives would intertwine again in the years ahead in ways none of us could have imagined.

CHAPTER 8
"DESTINED TO BE FRIENDS-
THE MCKENNEY FAMILY"

One day a letter arrived at the hospital addressed to Jim. It was from a former military friend of ours, Tom McKenney, who had been our next door neighbor when Jim was with the army at Ft. Campbell, Kentucky. I had informed the McKenneys of Jim's accident.

Jim had been drafted into the Army four months after his internship in Atlanta. With his medical degree, he entered the Army with the rank of captain. He had opted to train as a medical paratrooper rather than go to Korea and was stationed at Ft. Campbell, KY., home of the 101st Airborne Division. Ever the adventurous one, Jim was excited about being a paratrooper. It was rigorous training during a terrible heat wave that summer of 1956. I thought he would die from heat stroke but finally he graduated and went on to make more than twenty parachute jumps in the next two years.

One thing I didn't like about military life was the daily "Happy Hour" at the Officers' Club. Captain Tanner was always there. He could not hold his liquor well and did more than his share of partying and getting drunk.

I found this period in our marriage quite trying, but knew he would be out in two years.

Our third child was born while we were at Ft. Campbell, a son- Kenneth Moreland Tanner, June 8, 1957. Jim had unusual "duty" that summer. He's probably the only doctor that was on special duty to play baseball. He was a great pitcher and had once been considered for a position with the St. Louis Cardinals. Here he was, pitching for the 506th military baseball team. On the very day we were to bring our son home from the hospital Jim was pitching in an important game against a team from Ft. McClelland, Georgia. The base newspaper carried the following headline the next day: "Dr. Tanner gives Ft. McClelland the ether treatment!"

New neighbors moved into the apartment next to us. We shared the same porch stoop. Tom McKenney says that the first Tanner he ever saw was the infant Kenny in a bassinet near our front door, soaking up some sunshine. It was the weekend of July 4th, a date that would be important to our two families in years to come.

Tom and his wife, Marty, had two children, a daughter, Melissa, and a son, Jeff who was less than a year old. Although Ft. Campbell was an Army base, there was a small detachment of Marines there for special security measures. Tom was a captain in this Marine detachment.

We were casual neighbors, as military families often are. We shared a few meals, played a few games of bridge and visited back and forth. There was something about Tom that made me feel I already knew him, though we had never met. Now, I realize it was a spiritual kinship that was yet to be realized.

Tom was interested in parachute jumping and got special permission to enroll in jump school there. He was the first Marine to do so. Jim Tanner passed along the information to the Airborne cadre trainers that a Marine was going to go through the jump school program. "You're not going to let a Marine make it through the 101st Airborne School, are you? Besides," Jim lied, "He's an Olympic runner and will just laugh at you." It wasn't that Jim did not like Tom, it was just his idea of a good joke.

The trainers made it unbelievably tough on Tom; in fact, they were determined that no Marine would ever make it through the 101st Airborne jump school. Tom proved them wrong, of course and gained their respect. We remained friends during the remainder of our tenure.

As our two year stint in the army drew to a close, we made plans to move to Laurel, Mississippi where Jim would do a one year residency at the South Mississippi Charity Hospital. He was feeling out of touch with medicine after the past two years and felt he needed a refresher course. Also, he needed time to decide what he wanted to do concerning his medical practice. Laurel was only thirty miles from my home town and I was quite happy to be near my relatives again.

The McKenneys and Tanners kept in touch through Christmas cards but never personal letters, until the one that arrived at the hospital in Mobile that summer of 1961. It was a beautiful letter full of encouragement. Tom, of course, expressed his dismay over Jim's accident and pointed out his strong points, in that he had a brilliant mind, was well educated and had a tough constitution. He also said something else in that letter that I personally needed to hear. "One reason I feel so confidant about you, Jim, is that you have one wife in several million and she will help you through this."

If a person as nice as Tom McKenney had that much confidence in my ability to help Jim through this crisis, it was indeed a high compliment. Oh, how I needed uplifting! I had never felt lower in my life, yet I knew I needed to be stronger than I had ever been. We would not hear from the McKenneys except through the Christmas cards for over three more years.

CHAPTER 9

"THE REHAB DAYS"

Visitors didn't come to see Jim as much. I think it was partly because they couldn't bear to see him in such dreadful condition. The hospital chapel was still my source of refuge. I'd been a daily Bible reader since a teenager and the scriptures were a great consolation to me during this time. It was hard, however, to keep my mind off my many problems. The continual rain added to my despondency. The words to a poem I had memorized in high school came to mind often. "The Rainy Day" by Henry Wadsworth Longfellow, was one of the few poems that I could remember in its entirety. It expressed the emotions I was going through, but also offered me hope:

The day is cold and dark and dreary;
It rains, and the wind is never weary;
The vine still clings to the moldering wall,
But at every gust the dead leaves fall,
And the day is dark and dreary.

My life is cold, and dark and dreary;

It rains, and the wind is never weary;
My thoughts still cling to the moldering past,
But the hopes of youth fall thick in the blast,
And the day is dark and dreary.

Be still sad heart and cease repining;
Behind the clouds is the sun still shining;
Thy fate is the common fate of all,
Into each life some rain must fall,
Some days must be dark and dreary.

I especially like the phrase "Behind the clouds is the sun still shining…" It is a true statement with hope for anyone's situation.

Jim's doctors began to talk about sending him to a rehabilitation center. They had done all they could to help him and physical therapy would be the next course of treatment. After ten and a half weeks in Mobile Infirmary, Jim was transferred to the Rotary Rehabilitation Center, also in Mobile. They were not looking forward to having this ornery doctor as a patient. His reputation as an uncooperative patient preceded him.

I would not be able to see as much of Jim at the rehab center. He was to be in a ward with three other men in similar conditions. It was almost time for school to start for our children, and I needed to get back to Leakesville to get things ready. In this respect, the timing was good. It would be nice to have some sense of normalcy again for the children and myself, to sleep in my own bed again, away from the smell of the hospital, the sickness and despair.

Rehab was a big adjustment for Jim. Even though I made the sixty mile trip to visit him several times a week and every weekend, he missed me and wanted me by his side. The staff decided that a weekend away from the center would be good for him. He was not yet able to travel to Leakesville, so it was decided to try a weekend at his parents' house in Mobile.

It was so exciting to think of being together again, to sleep in the same bed, to be able to hold each other. Jim was still extremely weak and prone to fainting when he sat up, but he was trembling with excitement at being able to get away from the rehab center. I was excited too, but also scared at the idea of having to take care of him by myself.

I became a care-giver before I even knew the meaning of the word, or before it became a household term. I knew absolutely nothing about caring for a paraplegic. Although Jim was getting more use of his hands and arms, he still had no strength. He could not move his legs or wiggle a toe. Paralyzed from the waist down meant no bladder or bowel control. The catheter tube and bedside drainage bag would now be my responsibility. So also, would be the job of dressing and undressing him. I was given very little instruction about any of these things and didn't know exactly what to expect.

I was willing to try anything, do anything just to be with him, though my heart was full of fear and trepidation. Jim's parents' house was small and the bedroom crowded. We could barely get the wheelchair next to the bed. But finally he was in bed and I could lay beside him for the first time in many months.

It was wonderful to hold each other in our arms, to hug and kiss and renew our love. There was the very strong desire on both us to make love, but the sad reality was that the paralysis had taken its toll on Jim's sexual ability. We both cried. I reassured him that it didn't matter, things would get better in time. We were together and that's all that mattered, and it was true. I truly believed this was a temporary situation. For Jim with his medical knowledge, it was the realization of his worst fears.

I couldn't begin to imagine what it was like for him, to lose his manhood at only thirty years old, not to mention his ability to walk. Depression came over him like a wet blanket. Nothing I could do seemed to help. He knew too well what his prognosis was while I was hanging on as the eternal optimist. I reassured him of my undying devotion. I meant it and he needed to hear it.

We were both relieved when it was time for him to go back to the rehab center. Jim was feeling insecure in my ability to properly care for him. I felt the same, so afraid that I would do something wrong. I could not even begin to think down the road, how or if I could cope with caring for him when he came home for good. Physically, I was not feeling well either. It was apparent that something was wrong with the baby I was carrying or with me. I had buried my physical feelings, my emotions, my frustrations and worries in order to concentrate all my energies on Jim. My life, like his, was indeed dark and dreary.

To add to the emotional weekend for us, we were paid a visit at the Tanners' home by two men representing the insurance company of the other party involved in the accident. They wanted to settle the medical claims as quickly as possible. Later, we realized they wanted to settle for the medical liability on the policy before we took any action about suing them for long term disability. They made threats to the effect that they would try to prove Jim was driving the car and had already engaged an important attorney to take the case. The whole thing was a lie, which we could easily prove because of so many eye witnesses. However, the whole incident was terribly unnerving for both of us and we were in desperate need of financial help. The hospital was breathing down our necks for payment, the Rehab center had to be paid, and our personal fiancés were in disarray. Any litigation on our part would only delay any kind of settlement. The only lawyer I had talked to had already been dealing with the other insurance company, so we didn't know where to turn. With no one to advise us, we simply settled for the basic liability and that was the end of it. I have often wondered how those two agents felt when they walked out the door realizing what we faced in the future and knowing they could have made things easier for us.

We settled into a routine of the children and me living in Leakesville, making regular trips to Mobile to see Jim and living at his parents' home on weekends in order to be with him. The children were so glad to be back home in Leakesville and life was easier for me, except for the constant financial worries. I had long since written to our creditors to beg for extensions of our indebtedness. They were most understanding and agreed to postpone payments to a later date. I had already returned one of our two cars to the dealer as I could not afford the payment. I began to wish that we didn't have anything that wasn't paid for, even my beloved piano.

It was not that we were extravagant. We didn't own a lot of fine furniture and our lifestyle was simple. Jim had only been in private practice two years. We had built a simple cinder block clinic building, furnished it with the simplest furnishings and equipment, and were renting a house that we hoped to buy. We were making all our financial obligations until the bottom fell out of our little world.

Times were so hard that I found myself checking Jim's old coat and pants pockets to search for loose change to buy milk and bread. I was finally forced to borrow money from my father until we received the insurance settlement. Jim's parents had no savings The strain and stress of the past few months had taken a toll on my health. I had lost weight and a visit to my obstetrician in Mobile revealed that the child I was carrying was no longer living. "It's probably a blessing in disguise," the doctor told me," You're going to have your hands full taking care of your husband." How could he say such a thing, blessing in disguise? We wanted this child- desperately – it would probably be our last.

"What should I do?" I asked the doctor.

"It is better to let nature take its course." He replied, "You will go into labor and it will pass." My head was reeling. I had always had healthy, normal pregnancies. I realized that I was carrying a dead fetus inside my body, but for how long? What if I became infected? How would I know when the time came? I was so afraid, and I needed my husband to be with me.

I had to break the news to Jim and he didn't receive it well. He cried, we cried together. It was yet another hard blow. Jim sank deeper into depression and became physically ill. He was already battling urinary infections and a stubborn bedsore that had kept him in bed and delayed his rehabilitation. He trembled and shook uncontrollably.

Back home in Leakesville, the townspeople were wonderful to me. I often thought that if this tragic accident had happened when we lived in larger cities, even my next door neighbors might not have known about it. But here everyone cared and reached out with love and compassion. They filled our freezer with all kinds of food, meats, vegetables, enough to lasts for months. Friends would drop by with a cake or pie. When the public became aware of our dire financial situation, they organized a fund-raising event which they called "Dr. Tanner Day". People came from all over the county to eat barbeque, beans, salads and desserts. Someone bottled a special hot pepper sauce and labeled it "Tanner's Tonic". People were extremely generous and over $1500 was raised toward Jim's medical expenses.

The organizers had planned to pick Jim up in an ambulance from the rehab center and bring him to Leakesville for the event, but at the last minute he spiked a high fever and was unable to make the trip. While I was greatly appreciative of this wonderful out-pouring of financial blessing, it was hard to acknowledge that we were in need of charity. Truly, it was the hand of God at work. "Every good and perfect gift is from the Father of lights...." (James 1:17) I was feeling all along the words of Jesus when He said, "It is more blessed to give than to receive." (Acts 20:35)

My parents were concerned that I might go into labor alone at home, with no one to care for me, and there were signs that it might be imminent. My mother came to stay with me. I loved having her with me. She had always been there for me, no matter what and was a source of strength and comfort to me. She was there a week and nothing had happened, so she took advantage of an unexpected ride home to check on Daddy and get some clothes. As fate would have it, that was the very day I began hemorrhaging; not too bad at first, but by 10 o'clock that night I knew I needed to get to the hospital. I called a friend to come stay with the children and drove myself the two miles to the hospital. I can never recall feeling so alone in my life. I was hurting, I was scared and I wanted my husband's arms around me.

They took excellent care of me at the Greene County Hospital. It was over in a few hours but they kept me a day to rest. They never told me what the baby's sex was, so I have that surprise awaiting me in Heaven.

Someone had notified Jim of my miscarriage. He called me on the phone and was very sad. Afterwards, he went into shock and had a major setback. As soon as possible I went to see him. He perked up when he saw that I was well and healthy again. We had survived yet another crisis.

Jim was still not eating well. We had spoiled him at the hospital by carrying in fast food. The rehab center did not cater to the eating whims of their residents for obvious reasons, there were too many with overwhelming problems. One Sunday Jim had some special visitors. Our former housekeeper, nursemaid and cook, Paralee, and her husband, Ernest, came bearing a picnic basket full of Jim's favorite foods. Paralee was like a member of the family to us. Her grandmother had been a slave cook, and she, herself, had cooked in a boarding house before coming to work for us. Cooking was truly her gift. She hardly knew how to cook for a small family. When she made lemon pies, she made two or three, she didn't just fry one chicken, but several. She baked hot biscuits and homemade rolls by the dozens. When the accident happened, I had to let her go, and it broke my heart.

Her picnic basket held fried chicken, field peas, fresh corn, lemon pies, homemade rolls and sweet tea. Jim was propped up in bed and to everyone's surprise began to eat heartily. It pleased Ernest and Paralee so much and it proved to be a turning point for Jim.

This couple was dear to our hearts and to the hearts of our children. She had taken care of Kenny since he was eighteen months old and had spoiled him by holding him on her lap and spoon-feeding him. He loved her so much that if she left our house in the afternoon without him kissing her goodbye, I had to track her down, which was usually at the post-office, so he could kiss her. She took great pride in working for the new town doctor. I'd never had it so good. She did the cleaning, cooking, laundry and a lot of the child sitting. She liked for me to "dress up" when I worked at the clinic or went to town. One day I was going to the local grocery store to pick up a loaf of bread and was dressed in a pair of summer shorts. "Oh, no, Mrs. Tanner, you can't go to town like that."

"Why not?" I asked.

"You's the doctor's wife, you's got to look nice. Now get youself in there and change your clothes."

Of course, I did.

At the rehab center Jim began to make new friends, especially his room-mates. Two of them were in worse condition than he was. One, Leonard Chapman, had the exact same injuries as Jim and also had received them in an automobile accident. They were almost the same age and bonded quickly. Jim's sense of humor was starting to return after being around these fellows for a while. He and Leonard began pulling pranks on some of the nurses, like putting laxative pills in their cups of coffee. I met

Leonard's wife and son, and the two families became lasting friends.

Physical therapy was grueling but Jim worked hard. There was much at stake. Progress is sometimes painstakingly slow and it is easy to become discouraged. Set-backs are common and demoralizing. Jim had lost so much muscle tone in his arms and hands and what little use he had in his shoulders. Added to the physical therapy, was occupational therapy. He was taught to make leather bracelets, wallets, key-chains; anything to help increase the dexterity of his hands. Imagine a man of his intellect and medical degrees applying his time in such a way. It paid off in time, with a gradual return of strength to his arms and hands. The legs were another story. They did not respond to any kind of therapy or stimulation.

The visits to see Jim at the rehab center were not very pleasant for our children. There was not a good place to sit and visit, no privacy, and most of the residents were in as bad or worse condition than Jim. The one thing that brought them pleasure, other than seeing their father, was watching the beautiful dancing water fountain outside the front of the building. At night the fountain was lit with changing colors and held their attention for long periods of time. When it was time for us to leave, Jim would sink into depression.

CHAPTER 10

"JIM'S FIRST WEEKEND HOME"

After more than five months, Jim had progressed to the point where his doctors were letting him come home for the weekend! When the news got out the whole town was excited. Some people called to see if Dr. Tanner could see them as patients. Others called to see if there was anything they could do to help. We needed a wooden ramp into the main section of the house. We had converted our garage into a family room which was on the ground level. The ramp was a labor of love from Jim's friends and was solidly built.

I set about cleaning the house thoroughly. I knew Jim wouldn't notice or care, but I figured we'd have lots of visitors. I planned menus that would please Jim and engaged Paralee to come in and help with the cooking.

The big day finally arrived. The children and I could hardly contain our excitement. The girls were in school, but Kenny, only four, was home with me. I planned my grocery shopping for late morning, left a note for Paralee and the door unlocked so she could get in. When Kenny and I returned, she met me at the front door with a distraught look. "Oh, Mrs. Tanner! You won't believe what happened. It's terrible!" I feared something had happened to Jim. My heart began to race.

"What is it, Paralee? What on earth is wrong?"

She led me into the house, "You have to see for yourself." As I entered the kitchen carrying a bag of groceries, I saw what she meant. There in the middle of the kitchen table was a pile of yard dirt, about the size and shape of a child's sand-bucket.

"There's more, Mrs. Tanner." Indeed, there was. There was another pile of dirt in the middle of the dining room table that I had so lovingly polished only hours before. "That's not all," Paralee said. On the living room sofa, on one of the bunk beds, and in the middle of our own bed were bucket shaped piles of dirt. Shock was my immediate reaction, then anger. It was easy to see that a child's sand bucket had been used to perform the dirty work. But who would have done such a thing, and why? Only one answer came to my mind, the next door neighbors' two little boys, both under the age of six. Both parents worked and the children were supposed to be in the care of the housekeeper. Obviously, she had not done a good job of watching the boys.

I told Paralee not to clean anything up until I could speak to the father who usually came home for lunch. I went next door to talk to the maid. Since I had no proof that the boys were the culprits, I only told her to send Mr. Miller over when he came in for lunch.

For the life of me, I could not understand how they could have done so much damage in such a short time. There had been only a few minutes between the time I left, and the time Paralee arrived. True, I had left the door unlocked, but then most people around Leakesville rarely locked a door.

When Mr. Miller came over and saw the dirty deeds, his face got redder and redder and his eyes had fire in them. He headed for the peach tree in the yard and broke off the biggest switch on it. The boys were guilty, of course, but before it was all over I felt sorry for them because of the severity of their discipline. In my opinion, the sitter deserved some type of discipline.

Looking back, it was kind of funny except for the fact that I now realize it had been instigated by the devil to wreck havoc of my wonderful plans for Jim's homecoming. I was not as wise to his treacherous tricks as I am today. The boys, themselves, didn't know why they had done it. The parents were embarrassed beyond words, but we remained friends despite it all.

Jim's brother, Bill, had agreed to drive Jim from Mobile to Leakesville for the weekend and was supposed to help me care for him, since I would need a man's strength to help lift him. He was still weak and emotional about coming home. They arrived in the late afternoon and Bill got Jim out of the car and onto the daybed in the family room. He left, saying he would see us later. It was later, alright, two days later. I didn't know that, of course, and kept expecting him all evening. Jim was quite tired and ready for bed. Fortunately, Dr. Faulk, the other town doctor happened to drop by and helped me get him into bed.

How wonderful for Jim to be in his own bed again, to cuddle his children and have them give him kisses. Finally we were alone, in our own bedroom, but things were not the same, nor would they ever be again. We missed the intimacy so very much. Again, I assured Jim of my love and that being together was more important than anything else in life. And in my heart, I really meant it. I was absolutely certain that he would be well again, he would walk again, everything would return to normal.

I'm glad I was so optimistic, so naïve. It helped Jim and it helped me. If I had known the whole story, I would not have been able to handle it. Hope is a wonderful thing; it can keep you going when the going gets tough. Realizing how little he could do for himself, and how difficult it was for me, was extremely frustrating for Jim. Depression began to overshadow his joy at being home, making things even harder for me. Over and over, I kept reassuring him how happy I was to take care of him, and never once complained. Inside, I was a nervous wreck.

The children were not themselves that weekend. They seemed disturbed because it was obvious their father was not the same as before. Friends and patients of Jim's dropped by to visit, some bearing small gifts or a nice dessert. At least two people stuck money into his shirt pocket, two $100 bills, wow! It was a godsend. We drove Jim to the clinic, his old office, but it further depressed him. However, it uplifted him to know that his patients were anxious to have him treat them again. Some called to say that they realized he might not be able to see them, but if he would call in a prescription for them, they would pay him. It was good to know his patients still trusted and needed him.

Sunday afternoon arrived and so did Jim's brother, Bill. His explanation was that he had met up with some old friends and decided to hang out with them. The two left for Mobile and the rehab center. I was alone with the children to recoup from the weekend while I pondered many things about the future in my heart.

News of Jim's return home swept through the town and with it a barrage of phone calls and questions. "Is it true Dr. Tanner is returning to practice?" "Can I get an appointment to see Dr. Tanner?" It was becoming clear that his patients were anxious to have him as their doctor again, regardless of the wheelchair. Jim was so encouraged that he planned to come home again the following weekend.

Soon he was coming home every weekend and I was his means of transportation. One of Jim's best friends, Lavon Reese was coming around to help out. He had avoided visiting Jim in the hospital because he could not bear to see his good buddy in such a condition. Jim had nicknamed Lavon "Wormy" because he was thin and wiry, but in reality he was as strong as an ox and could pick Jim up with one arm. He was a tremendous help to me and was good for Jim because he joked with him and would not let him feel sorry for himself. He took a personal interest in seeing that Jim had the best of care and became his personal attendant.

Soon Jim was seeing patients every Saturday that he was home. It was good for his morale and certainly good for our finances. Now, for the most part, people paid their bills, instead of charging them. Jim continued to spend the weekdays at the rehab center undergoing therapy. Gradually, he became stronger and could stay up longer hours. He was fitted for a body brace that reached from under his arms all the way down to his feet. Made of stainless steel, and hinged at the hips and knees, the braces weighed about sixty pounds. For my one hundred five pound frame, they were a heavy load. Eventually, I was able to handle the braces and get his clothes on over them. I also learned to fold and lift the wheelchair which was quite heavy. Added to this was my responsibility of keeping the house, doing the cooking, caring for the children, handling the finances, etc. My strength and nerves were often stretched to the limit.

It was the best of times and the worst of times. It was good to be back together as a family, but it was difficult to care for Jim in our inconvenient house. Our bathroom door was too narrow for the wheelchair to go through and could not be enlarged because of the arrangement of the tub and cabinets. Finally I resorted to an old office chair on rollers, but I had to lift Jim's legs and drag him and the chair through the bathroom door. There was the regular routine of bowel and bladder management which was quite difficult.

Jim made the decision to come home to live full time and make twice weekly trips to Mobile for therapy. The problem was that he could not manage this by himself and I could not take on any more than I was already carrying. He and Lavon worked out a plan. Lavon would come to work for us on a full time basis at the same salary he was drawing at the local hospital where he was a lab technician. He would drive Jim to Mobile, help with his therapy, take him to the clinic and to make hospital rounds. It was a big load for Lavon but he was willing to do this for his best friend. We needed a second car now, which we managed with the help of some of the insurance money. It was a red Chevy II two door sedan, no frills, no air conditioning, but the wheelchair would fit in the trunk or between the front and back seats. That car would serve us for the next fifteen years.

Uncertainty about our future was eating away at me. How long could Jim hold up under such a load? Lavon pushed Jim hard to new levels of therapy. Jim learned to "walk" with crutches and the braces by swinging his body from the shoulders down. He still had no movement from the chest down, so he wasn't really walking at all, just swinging through with Lavon holding onto to him to keep him from losing his balance. It looked like progress, but it wasn't. It required immense concentration on Jim's part, far too taxing on his strength.

Bouts of depression would hit him at times, usually when we were home at night. Instead of watching TV with the family, he would turn his face toward a blank wall and hang his head. I tried to encourage him, at the same time battling my own emotions. They had told me at the rehab center to try to keep our home life as normal as possible, and above all to not let him indulge in self-pity. One evening during one of his periods of depression, I said. "I know how you feel."

His anger flared, "Oh, no you don't! You just think you do. You have no idea!"

Something inside of me rose up. I had bottled up my feelings for months on end. It all came out. I had not had a normal day since the accident. "You think you've had it rough? What do you think about me? I'm the one who has had to hold everything together, worrying about you, the children, where the money was coming from, losing the baby......" My nerves had been stretched to the limit!

I cried uncontrollably. Jim looked as though I had slapped his face. His countenance changed, he lifted his shoulders and from that time on he seemed different, more determined, more considerate. The old fighting spirit was back, even though he still had moments of discouragement.

So, where was God in all this? Sometimes it's hard to know in the middle of a valley. Jesus is the lily of the valley, and he was there all the while, gently guiding and planning for us. I remember one night when I couldn't sleep for worrying, looking up at the moon shining through the boughs of a pine tree outside our bedroom, and praying as fervently as I have ever prayed. "God, if you don't want us to continue on this present course, if you have another direction for us, please, please let us know."

Chapter 11

"Country Doctor"

Country doctors are a unique breed. Some people consider them their personal property, expecting them to jump when called. They do lay aside their private lives in order to accommodate their patients. True public servants, often too much is expected of them. The fact that Jim was practicing medicine from a wheelchair didn't alter that fact much. His patients, however, did not expect him to make house calls in the middle of the night as he had formerly done. They came to our house instead. At times our house was like an open clinic. I often walked into the family room to find patients sitting there waiting for the doctor to come in. Our lives were not our own

It was not unusual for the doorbell to ring at all hours of the day or night. One night we were awakened by the persistent ringing of the bell. As I answered the door a black lady stood there holding a limp infant who was wheezing so hard it could hardly breathe. The child was having a severe asthmatic attack and the mother was frantic. Jim was in bed, of course, and it would take a while to get him dressed and up. "You'll have to give the baby a shot of ephedrine, Ouida," he said.

I was mortified; I had never given a shot of anything to anyone at anytime. I couldn't possibly stick a needle into a tiny baby! "I can't do it, Jim, please don't ask me." There was no time to lose he insisted, as he gave me specific instructions as to how much medicine, the right size syringe and needle, how many CCs to draw from the vial, where on the baby's buttocks to make the injection.

I was used to handling needles and syringes as I often cleaned and autoclaved them for sterilization in the clinic. But I was trembling as I responded to Jim's instructions. Almost instantly, the gasping and wheezing stopped, the baby relaxed and the mother gave a huge sigh of relief. Not nearly as huge as my own, I might add.

There were too many experiences to recount, like sewing up a cut foot on the coffee table; but one experience really stands out. The phone rang around 2:00 A.M. and a man's frantic voice said, "Is Dr. Tanner there? My wife is real sick."

"Can you bring her here? "I asked.

"I'll be right there." Click! I woke Jim and told him he would have to get up and reached for his trousers to dress him. The doorbell rang. It had not been three minutes. The young man had been just around the corner when he called. As I opened the door, he stood there with his wife in his arms.

"Where is he?" he demanded.

"He's still in the bed," I responded. Brushing me aside, down the hall he went carrying his wife and proceeded to drop her in the bed with Jim! No need to get up now. Jim propped up on one elbow and began to examine the young woman, asking questions. As it turned out, they were newlyweds and the situation was not very serious. He wrote a prescription and they went on their way. We teased him about his bedside manner after that.

Jim had always had a great relationship with his patients. He was a great teaser and sometimes the patients didn't know whether he was serious or not. Such was the case with some prenatal vitamins that he gave his maternity patients. They were capsules, pink on one end and baby blue on the other end. Jim told some of his patients that if they wanted a girl, they must swallow the pink end first, or the blue end first if they wanted a boy. Occasionally, a lady would come in and say, "Dr. Tanner, I did just what you said. I was careful to swallow the blue end first, but I had a girl."

The medical practice was growing; too much, in fact. Jim had decided not to take any obstetric cases because of his obvious handicap. However, one day there was an emergency situation at the hospital. A lady was in labor and Dr. Faulk was out of town. The hospital called desperately needing help, could Jim please come? Lavon loaded him and the wheelchair in the car and away they went to the rescue, not knowing whether or not he could meet the challenge. As we jokingly say, everything came out alright. The next day there were three new maternity cases in the clinic waiting room. In the ensuing months Jim probably delivered as many as fifty babies from the wheelchair. But he was troubled that one day he might not successfully be able to deliver a child. What if the mother needed a C-section? It was too risky for everyone concerned.

Jim began to realize that some changes needed to take place. About this time his old friend, Dr. Howard Thomas contacted him, asking if he needed some help in his practice. He had lost his job as a physician with a copper mining company in Arizona and was available. Jim was aware that Howard still had a problem with drug addiction, but wanted to help him and had his own need for help in the clinic. Howard was a brilliant doctor, even when on drugs, but of course there was great concern on our part. They decided to give it a trial of a month to see if it would work out.

It was great at first. Howard lived in our home, sharing Kenny's room. His family would come later if things worked out. As the days passed, we became suspicious that Howard was still on the drugs and he kept late and irregular hours. Jim talked with him and was assured things were fine. Then one day, we intercepted a package intended for Howard— an order of narcotics. He had to be confronted. Jim always said that the hardest thing he ever had to do was to tell his best friend that he would have to leave. They both cried. It was a sad scene.

In my heart I knew that God could deliver Howard from his addiction, but I wasn't sure how to go about witnessing to him or whether or not he would listen. I have regretted many times that I did not pursue the matter.

God did not give up on Howard, however, and the next time we would see him, he would be a changed man.

If Jim had a hobby, it was fishing. He loved it and when he was on his feet he would carry a rod and reel in the car and try to sneak in a few minutes of fishing when he was out on house calls. The accident put a stop to that, but one day Lavon decided it was time they gave fishing a try. They were going to fish from a boat in a river. I had another one of those ominous feelings and was quite worried.

" Don't you dare get in the boat without a life-preserver," I cautioned. I didn't see how Lavon could possibly get Jim down the embankment, into a boat by himself, no-matter how strong he was. I prayed and prayed, but the uneasiness wouldn't go away.

When they weren't home by dark, I was panicky. Just as I was about to send out a search party, the doorbell rang. There were two of the muddiest, grayest looking creatures you ever saw, and one of them was in a wheelchair. "What happened?" I cried.

They told me the details of how the boat turned over dumping Jim into the murky water. Jim's version was that he felt himself sinking into the bottom of the river, feet down, with the heavy metal braces sticking in the mud. As he expressed it, "I felt the grim reaper had me for sure." Suddenly, he felt a strong hand grab the brace from the back of his shoulders and with a mighty thrust lifted him up so that his head was above water. Jim was unable to help himself because of his paralysis, so it was up to Lavon to rescue him.

Somehow they managed to reach the boat, with Jim hanging on for dear life. When they finally reached the river bank, Jim said, "Thank the Lord!" to which Lavon replied, "Thank the Lord, the devil, I'm the one who pulled you out." They had some good laughs about it later. I saw no humor in it whatsoever.

And guess who got to clean up the slimy mess? You guessed it. I padded the bed with thick quilts and slowly got the muddy clothes and braces off. The shoes were full of mud also. They didn't want to admit they had not used life preservers, but it was obvious.

We took the days one at a time and there were many problems, adjustments and times of discouragement. Leakesville was a very small town of about a thousand people. There wasn't much to do, or see, so we often went for drives in the country. One spring day the weather was unusually beautiful as we drove along a stretch of lovely countryside. We crossed a bridge covering a sparkling creek, so clear you could see the bottom and almost sense the fish jumping. Jim made a remark that caused a lump in my throat and tore at my heart. It summed up the deep longing in his heart to be able to use his legs again. "I could walk a country mile down that creek," he wistfully said. Thus, this book's name.

The day finally came after two years in the wheelchair that we made one of the most important decisions of our lives. Jim decided to give up his medical practice and enter another field of medicine.

While he was a patient at the rehab center in Mobile, they had encouraged him to consider going into the field of Rehabilitation Medicine, to become a physiatrist, a specialist in spinal cord injuries and other disabilities. It was a relatively new field at the time. There were very few physiatrists in the country. The rehab center offered to give Jim a permanent job when he completed the three years of training. Jim inquired about openings for residencies in the field. There would be an opening in Richmond, Virginia the following summer. The training program would be between the McGuire Veterans Administration Hospital and the University of Virginia Medical College. Jim made application.

It was hard to think of leaving the security of Leakesville, of living near both sets of our parents and other relatives, our many friends and church family. I was particularly worried about moving a thousand miles away with a handicapped husband and three small children. We were embarking on a new adventure that would require all the courage we could muster.

CHAPTER 12
"A FRESH START: MOVING TO VIRGINIA"

Prior to our trip to Virginia for the interview, I sent off for some information on the city of Richmond. We had lived in a couple of large cities, Atlanta and Memphis, but we had never lived so far from home. My mind conjured up all kinds of scenarios as to where we might live and the housing situation. We had lived in public housing before and I was dreading the thought of that, especially after having our own house in quiet little Leakesville. I could envision crowded high-rise apartments along a busy freeway. I'd never worried too much about our previous moves because Jim was in charge and on his feet. Now, much would depend on me.

We took the children to my parents' house and headed northeast. It was also the first time we had been on an extensive trip since Jim's accident. I had to do all the driving as we did not have hand controls on the car. At last, we relaxed a little as we began to enjoy the unfolding scenery.

As we entered the city of Richmond, my heart sank. Almost as I had envisioned there were low-rent housing developments along the free-way near downtown, but to my great relief as we approached the Holiday Inn in the heart of town, things started to look infinitely better. After a good night's rest we headed toward the VA hospital and the interview. My spirits rose as we drove down beautiful Monument Avenue with its fine old town-houses and majestic monuments. Our route took us by the Virginia Museum of Fine Arts, the city park and its bell carillon, and across the Nickle bridge that spanned the stunningly beautiful James River. Its waters sparkled over majestic stone and rock. My eyes drank it all in. Maybe this move wouldn't be so bad after all.

The interview went well. The doctor in charge said that he wouldn't hesitate to hire Jim because of his handicap, but he would have to meet with the other members of the board, "Red Tape", he emphasized. After some reflection he said that since it was such a long way to Mississippi, perhaps it would be good to look at housing while we were there. "In fact," the doctor said, "I remember seeing a house listed on the bulletin board at the hospital that was designed for a wheelchair."

Looking back, it was almost like seeing Moses part the waters of the Red Sea for the Israelites in the movie The Ten Commandments. God was about to reveal Himself to us in ways we could never have imagined.

The notice about the house on the bulletin board, also had a sketch of the house and a floor plan. It truly had been designed for a wheelchair. It was in an area not too far from the hospital called Stratford Hills, which was near the beautiful James River. The coordinator of the PM & R Department of the hospital lived in the Stratford Hill area and offered to lead us there. We fell in love with the house and neighborhood instantly--rolling hills, tree-lined streets, neat homes. I couldn't believe it. The house was perfect; ground level, three bedrooms, living-dining combination, kitchen and den combination, two full baths and a covered carport. The yard was full of trees and flowers and there was even a tree house in the back yard.

The lady of the house, whose name was Joy, was in a wheelchair, and she was also an artist. It was all too good to be true. There was just one hitch--it was for sale, not for rent. What a disappointment, but the realtor was willing to work with us and took a small deposit to hold it for us. Jim still did not officially have the position and we were negotiating with a doctor to buy our clinic in Leakesville. If we could come up with a $1000 down payment, the house would be ours and our house notes would be cheaper than the house we had in Leakesville.

We were truly excited and didn't bother to look at any more houses. Why should we? God had met our every need. We left for Mississippi the next day.

Traveling in a wheelchair in 1963 was difficult. It was long before the days of required facilities for the disabled. Finding a room in a motel that had a wide bathroom door was almost impossible. Sometimes we had to drive an extra couple of hundred miles out of the way to find a place. It was extremely frustrating. Most people don't realize the barriers for people in wheelchairs. Something as simple as a low bed can create all kinds of problems. I became an expert at devising ways to accommodate Jim's needs, even to taking off his belt and hooking it around the wheelchair to make it more narrow in order to negotiate a bathroom door.

Back in Mississippi, we began finalizing our business. A young doctor was interested in taking over Jim's practice, but was just starting out and had no money. We had almost no equity in our clinic and equipment because of the postponement in our making regular payments. We did, however, realize enough money out of it to make the down payment on the house in Richmond and to help with our moving expenses.

There were some lovely surprises awaiting us when we arrived in Richmond. The neighborhood had much to offer. There was a school a block away for the children, a neighborhood recreation center two blocks away with an Olympic sized pool, an outdoor ice skating rink, and other amenities. There was a Methodist church two blocks away. Our backdoor neighbor was a veteran in a wheelchair. Another neighbor who lived across the street was also in a wheelchair, an amputee. Furthermore, Jim could carpool with the fellow who was the coordinator of the PM&R department where he would be working. God thought of everything!

Our neighbors were wonderful- so genteel and friendly. There was even a couple from Mississippi close by. The weather was a refreshing change from the hot, humid summers of the deep south. We looked forward to seeing snow in the winters- something we had rarely seen.

The children and I visited the Methodist church and were promptly visited at home. The pastor told me not to mention it to Jim but they were going to build a ramp for him so he could easily access the church. Soon, we had a new church home and a new church family. God was pouring on the blessings. We didn't always give him the credit and certainly not the praise He deserved. We considered ourselves very "lucky".

In all the years of our marriage, we had never taken a real family vacation. Any free time we had was used up in visiting relatives, which was good, but now there was so much to see and do. We were within two hours of exciting places- the beautiful Blue Ridge Parkway and Skyline Drive, Monticello, Washington, D.C., Williamsburg and Jamestown, Virginia and the outer banks of North Carolina. We took advantage of these at relatively small costs. Most times we did not have to stay overnight, and took our own picnics. Jim's attitude improved, and so did his health. "A merry heart doeth good like a medicine." (Proverbs 17:22)

The neighborhood recreation center was such a blessing, especially to me. I was asked to teach art classes there. Even though I had never taught art classes before, I had prepared myself by taking a home correspondence course through the Famous Artists School in Westport, Connecticut and received my three-year diploma. Their textbooks were great and provided a good foundation for my teaching. The extra money was great. Although our finances were a little more secure, we were just barely getting by. With my art money we were able to purchase some dining room furniture which was the nicest furniture we had ever had.

I also did a few commissioned pastel portraits and became involved in an art league. I loved the culture of Virginia, so much history. It nourished me spiritually and emotionally. Trips to the local museum, to the National Gallery and Smithsonian in Washington, special exhibits of famous artists I had only read about--- it was all so wonderful to me. It helped so much to make up for the hard times and the fact that I still had the heavy responsibilities of taking care of my paraplegic husband. It was not exactly a bed of roses.

My role as a caregiver was never ending. Jim was still wearing the full length braces. I had to help get him in and out of the bathtub, as well as giving him daily exercises by stretching his legs and rotating his hips so that his limbs did not become distorted. There was the ongoing problem of bowel and bladder care, but we settled into a routine and the burden didn't seem nearly so difficult as it had once been.

From time to time Jim would resort to periods of depression and say hurtful things to me. It was eating away at him that he could no longer perform sexually. "I know you want a man," he would lash out at me, "Go ahead and get yourself one. I can take it." It hurt me for him to think that I would ever do such a thing. I had never given him cause to speak like that. What I really heard him saying was, "Reassure me of your love." And I did, over and over again. In reality, it was hard for me to give up this aspect of our lives. I missed the intimacy. I was only twenty-eight at the time of the accident, and my hormones were in full swing. But I took my marriage vows seriously, and the words of Jesus regarding adultery. I would not hurt Jim by being unfaithful, nor would I lower my own standards.

Jim was quite happy in his residency program. He learned a lot about his own condition and was able to empathize with his patients. He was able to ward off a lot of potential problems such as bedsores, muscle contractions, etc. by knowing what to do or not to do. We had some parallel metal bars put up in the backyard so he could stand, with the help of the braces locked into position. This standing was important to his circulation. He had not yet wiggled a toe.

I continued to hold out hope that he would walk again. The three-year time frame that the rehab center had given him in Mobile to recover use of his legs was running out. As time ran out, my hopes dimmed, but I also knew that "Hey, we can make it anyway."

The children were so happy in our new home. They loved the tree house, made new friends, enjoyed the pool and even learned to ice skate. Most of all they loved the snow. We all enjoyed getting snow-bound. Jim couldn't get to work, so he and I played endless games of dominoes and sat by the open fireplace. The children sledded down the hills in the neighborhood, and made snowmen. Most of our neighbors played bridge and we spent many happy hours with them. Life was good.

We had a lot of out-of-town visitors, mostly relatives. It was easy to entertain them with all the great places to go and things to do. Our good friends, the Chapmans, of rehab center days came to visit. Leonard and

Jim did a lot of sight-seeing in their wheelchairs.

God was about to bring back across our paths another family from our past, an event that would forever change the course of our lives. Tom and Marty McKenney and their children from Ft. Campbell, Kentucky and the paratrooper days, had moved to Chapel Hill, North Carolina. Tom had taken Jim's advice to "go for it", had resigned from the Marine Corp. and had taken a teaching position in Greenville, Ohio. Now he was going to work on his master's degree at the University of North Carolina.

Thank God for Christmas cards! It was because we exchanged Christmas cards that we stayed in touch with each other and I found out that they would only be 150 miles from us. They hadn't seen Jim since the accident. We had shared a Thanksgiving dinner together in the old days, so I thought it would be nice to invite them to visit us during that holiday time, November of 1964. I cooked and cleaned and planned sight-seeing trips. The McKenneys were real history buffs and we filled the weekend with all kinds of exciting things. Our children got along famously.

Jim and Tom reminisced over paratrooper days and Marty and I caught up on the years between. She had the most beautiful brown eyes and the longest eye lashes I had ever seen. We had a bountiful Thanksgiving meal, which has always been Tom's favorite holiday- no gifts to buy, just a time for fellowship and thanksgiving. As they drove away that weekend, the McKenney children were hanging out of the car windows crying and the Tanner children were standing in the driveway crying. We all hated to part and agreed to visits more often.

And so began a time of real bonding between the two families who were never to be casual friends again, but more like family. They came as often as time allowed and we did a lot of wonderful things together- the mountains, Monticello, Washington, Williamsburg. Once the McKenneys got snow-bound while visiting, and we rejoiced. What fun the kids and even the adults had sledding down the many neighborhood hills.

Jim had a patient who owned a small motel in Kill Devil Hills on the outer banks of North Carolina, and he had offered us a free week there during the off season. Jim asked Mr. Cook, " How about a week for our friends, too?" He complied and we had a great time.

It was there on the outer banks that I fell in love with the ocean and painted my first seascape. The breeze was so strong that I had to anchor the legs of my easel to keep it from blowing over, but what a joy. The blowing sand stuck to my canvas, the salt air tantalized my senses, and I was having a hard time determining whether I liked the mountains or the ocean best.

It was in Richmond that I took up a new hobby: sculpture. I wasn't too pleased with the basic course I took, doing plaster relief pieces. I was eager to move on to the harder stuff, so I checked a book out of the library on sculpting heads, and proceeded to learn on my own. I bought unfired bricks, soaked them in water, made my own clay and decided to sculpt a bust of Jim. I was excited at the feel of the clay under my hands- it was three-dimensional, almost life-like. I built an armature on which to build up the clay. The head began to take place. I was working in our screened in carport in the summer time.

In order to make the form exact, I needed to measure Jim's head. He was in bed for the night, so I quietly got out my measuring tape and without touching him, began to calculate the dimensions. He opened his eyes and said, "What are you doing, measuring me for a coffin?"

My heart was racing as the image began to take shape under my fingers. The next day I looked at the completed head and felt a little bit like Michelangelo after he had completed the magnificent sculpture of David. He is quoted as having said, "Breathe, damn you, breathe!" I was quite proud of my creation even though it was just a work of clay. God is the only One who breathed into a mound of clay and it became life! As I stood there admiring my work, I noticed a little Z shape on the top of the head. In seconds it began to spread and then before my eyes half of the head fell off on one side, and the other half fell on the other side! All that work! I was crushed.

On closer observation, I realized the reason for the calamity. My armature, or framework, was not strong or secure enough. I had used a wooden post, wire and newspaper underneath, but it would not hold up under the weight of the heavy clay. I have often thought back on the sculpting experience as a spiritual lesson learned.

According to I Corinthians 3:10 and following: "Each should be careful how he builds....his work will be shown for what it is.....if what he has built survives, he will receive his reward...."vs. 14. This of course, refers to spiritual matters, to building our faith on the sure foundation of Jesus Christ. The Bible has a lot to say about building on a firm foundation. I am so thankful that though my faith was not full blown in those days, its roots were on a firm foundation.

I'm happy to say that I was not defeated by the sculpture disaster. I corrected the problem, built a more secure armature, and remodeled the head in clay. It was better in every way than before. I like to think I am better from the whole experience.

The time drew near when we would have to leave Richmond. I was dreading it. I had enjoyed living there more than any other place we had lived. Jim's residency program was nearly complete and he would be seeking a job in the field of Physical Medicine and Rehabilitation. He considered returning to Mobile, where he had been assured of a position with the Rotary Rehab Center. But he was also offered a position with the Veterans Administration Hospital in Durham, North Carolina, where he would also be affiliated with Duke University Hospital. It was a prestigious position, and we made two different trips to Durham to look for housing. Nothing was working out, unlike the clear unfolding of housing in Richmond. Jim didn't have a peace about the whole thing anyway. One consideration for staying with the VA system was the benefit package, primarily insurance coverage, something that is not readily available for disabled persons. We also had reservations about putting down roots so far from our families in Alabama and Mississippi.

Obviously, the Lord had other plans for us because He made a way for us to move to Memphis, Tennessee, where we had lived the last two years of medical school. A position was actually created for Jim as assistant director of the Physical Medicine and Rehabilitation Department of the Veterans Administration Hospital there, which was at that time located at Park and Getwell streets.

Moving day arrived and my heart was heavy. I had never been happier than those years in Richmond, despite Jim's condition. I loved the people, the area, our house. We chose a moving company out of the phone book-

TANNERS- we figured with a name like that it had to be good. The picnic table was the last thing to be packed, because our neighbors were gathered around it having a farewell party for us. They were toasting our departure with frosty mint juleps. Jim was feeling pretty good, but I was working too hard to participate.

Due to a set of unusual circumstance Tom McKenney was going to be able to drive one of our two cars to Memphis for us. He and his family had moved to Kentucky the year before, but at the present time he was still in the Marine Reserves and had to do some summer training at Quantico, Virginia. Jim would not have been able to drive the entire distance from Richmond to Memphis. Tom needed transportation back to Kentucky and we needed a driver to Memphis. God was still meeting our needs.

The truck was loaded, even the picnic table, and we said our tearful goodbyes to the greatest neighbors in the world. Some of those neighbors have remained good friends over the years and we have often visited one another. I took a last walk around the backyard I had grown to love so much- plucking a small spray of ornamental cherry blossoms to take with me. Tears trickled down my cheeks as I walked to the car and we headed west.

We were off on a new adventure and what an incredible venture it would be!

Chapter 13

"Moving to Memphis"

The little two-car caravan inched its way toward Memphis, Tennessee. The heat was brutal and traffic slowed to a crawl at times because of highway construction. Interstate 40 was in the process of being cut through the mountains of eastern Tennessee.

We had rented a house in Memphis, sight-unseen, over the phone through a realtor. When we arrived I was astonished at the size of it. It was huge! Its location on prestigious South Parkway was impressive, but not for long. The house was situated on a pie-shaped wedge of property at a major intersection with six lanes of traffic on one side of it and eight lanes of traffic on the other side. Noise was a big problem. No wonder there was a "High Accident Location" sign right by our driveway! Sirens blared night and day and we also realized we were on the glide path of the Memphis airport and near a busy railroad. What a far cry from our tranquil neighborhood in Richmond. We had no choice but to make the most of it.

We enrolled the children in local schools and Jim settled into his new job as assistant physician to the Chief of the Physical Medicine and Rehabilitation. He would be doing the job he had trained for the past three years. As for me, I began searching for another house.

One weekend as we were house-hunting, we found ourselves on the east side of Memphis in a small pretty neighborhood called Trafalger Village. The houses were all different and it was quiet, away from the endless traffic and noise. Eventually, we signed a contract with a builder for a wheelchair accessible house in that neighborhood. It was our first time to have a custom built home. I was especially happy because I got to select the carpet, wallpaper and paint.

During our frequent trips to check on the house construction, we passed a small church about a mile away called Good Shepherd United Methodist Church. I liked the name and decided to visit their Sunday services. Jim wasn't interested so I took the children with me. It was a small modern chapel with a separate cottage type building for Sunday School. The people were friendly and I felt at peace there. I was particularly impressed with the young pastor, Ed Horten , and his family.

Later I announced to Jim that I had found "my church". In time he joined us, saying that he liked the preacher because he had a crew-cut. Little did we know that we were about to embark on a spiritual journey that we could not have imagined!

Our new custom built house was wonderful. It was so much easier to care for Jim with the convenience of a wheel-chair friendly bathroom and a carport that kept him dry in the rain. We soon became involved in the small neighborhood community. Our children made new friends and settled into their schools. Our social life centered around the church and we found ourselves in leadership roles. Jim often remarked that he was made chairman of the Membership and Evangelism Committee before he understood what the term "evangelism" meant.

Jim was invited to attend a Methodist Men's Retreat by virtue of his status as "chairman" of the Evangelism committee. The retreat was to be held at Lambuth College in Jackson, Tennessee in September of 1967. Knowing that it would be almost impossible for him to manage his special needs as a paraplegic without my assistance, Jim decided to play along with the idea and then back out of it at the last minute. God, however, had other plans and he found himself being propelled right along to the retreat despite his protests.

Once there on the college's lovely campus, Jim said his worst fears were realized. There, in broad daylight, men were greeting each other with robust hugs and gathering in small groups to pray. He was leary of affectionate embraces between men and men. He was becoming more uncomfortable by the minute. The pivotal point of the weekend came in a small group discussion where each man was asked to make a graph on paper of his spiritual walk with the Lord. Jim put a little blip on his graph when he joined the Methodist church at twelve years old. After that there was no other high point. He found himself staring at the piece of paper and realizing that he was farther away from God at age thirty-seven than he was at age twelve.

He was further jolted when the group leader, Dr. Tom Shipman, a well respected dentist, asked him a profound and life changing question, "Jim, if you were to die tonight, where would you spend eternity? His defenses were down, he got brutally honest with himself.
"Well, Tom, if there is such a place as hell I would split it wide open."

Dr. Shipman replied, "It doesn't have to be that way, Jim. We can settle the issue right now." Jim found himself wheeling down the aisle to the altar of the little chapel where he had a divine encounter with Jesus Christ. This intelligent, well-educated medical doctor was not prone to exaggerations or hallucinations, yet over the years Jim Tanner never deviated from his account of that moment.

In his own words: There was Jesus, standing behind the railing, as real and alive as any human being and He spoke these words to me, "'Jim, I've been waiting for you all your life. Now, I'm going to make you into what you always wanted to be, but could never be on your own.'"

All his frustrations, struggles and fears seemed to subside in the loving presence of his Lord and Savior, Jesus Christ. It had been Jim's first weekend away from me as his caregiver. Upon his return he looked weary but peaceful as I prepared him for bed. Before he went to sleep he said, "Ouida, you are not number one in my life anymore." I knew what he meant, and I was elated. He had found something more precious than even a wife and children - a personal encounter with the King of Kings and Lord of Lords. His soul was secure and his name was written in the Lamb's Book of Life.

He began to read his Bible and was more involved in church activities. He radiated with new joy and peace. I liked the new Jim, but wondered if it would last.

When Jim suggested that we pray together as husband and wife, I knew he had indeed changed. Mostly we prayed together before we got out of bed in the early mornings, holding hands. This practice drew us closer to the Lord and each other for the remainder of our married life. Now we were spiritually joined together which was more intimate than anything we had experienced before.

CHAPTER 14

"SPIRITUAL JOURNEY"

God was working in our lives. Jim continued to grow in his faith and I found it contagious. I began my own search for a deeper walk with the Lord. I had always been a daily Bible reader, but I knew there was much more to the Christian walk than I was experiencing. God had already begun building our faith through a very unexpected source.

One afternoon we were paid a visit from our old and dear friends, Dr. Howard Thomas and his wife, Ann, the same friends who had been so heavily addicted to drugs many years before. We had more or less lost track of each other, especially with our moving several times. Here they were in our kitchen and I could hardly believe my eyes! The transformation was nothing short of a miracle. They were radiant, healthy looking and full of joy--nothing like the emaciated drug addicts when we had last seen them.

There was no doubt they had an experience of some kind. They had changed.—Ann's personal appearance and mode of dress had changed. She wore her hair in a bun on top of her head, no makeup and a dress almost to her ankles. She was still beautiful but very different from the Ann I had known.

As we listened to their story of the supernatural power of God that had set them free from years of unbelievable drug addiction, we knew it was divine intervention in their lives. After all, we had known them before, during, and after their addiction.

They spoke of things we had never heard before, like the baptism of the Holy Spirit, and speaking in unknown tongues. Whoa, hold on here.... this was getting pretty heavy. Yet here they were, totally transformed. How could we deny God's power!

When they left our house, Jim and I both marveled at how God was moving not only in Howard and Ann's lives, but in our own. We had a new hunger for the things of God, and the power of the Holy Spirit.

In May of 1968 our little church was becoming involved in a movement of evangelism that was called The Lay Witness Mission. Simple in strategy, yet powerful in results, it was basically a weekend in which a church invites a team of ordinary lay people into their midst to share their personal testimonies of how Jesus has made a difference in their lives. They were not to preach or teach but simply share from their personal experiences and show forth the love of God. In fact, the theme for the missions would be, "God loves you and I love you." Team members would be guests in the homes of the parishioners and there would be church-wide fellowship meals, coffee groups and small discussion groups. The group leader would also be a lay person, but one well trained to coordinate the event, which was to be bathed in prayer.

Jim and I were excited about the upcoming event and that our friends the Thomases had been invited. We volunteered to host them in our home along with a young teenage girl about the age of our two daughters. Other team members included an insurance agent, a banker and his wife, a hog farmer and his wife from Dresden, Tennessee, a school principal and others. We listened intently as one by one they shared their faith

Over the course of the weekend we got to know these wonderful people and felt their love. My heart was strangely warmed. They had such joy! They had such love! I felt like I was missing out on something special. I didn't know what, but I wanted what they had. I could not sleep on Saturday night and could hardly wait for the Sunday morning service. If anyone had asked me prior to that weekend if I had been "saved", I would have said

81

"Yes". But now I was under conviction that I wasn't sure of my salvation. I had been a church goer all my life, and at the present time had about ten different jobs in the church, hoping to earn my way into Heaven. What a tremendous relief it was when I read in the Bible, "For it is by GRACE you have been saved, through FAITH-and this not from yourselves, it is the gift of God- NOT BY WORKS, so that no one can boast." (Ephesians 2:8-9)

When the invitation came to go to the altar, I was the first one down there and on my knees. I looked around and there was Jim and then our daughters, Debby and Dawn. Our son Kenny was quite young at the time and did not understand what was happening. I shall never forget what I experienced in those moments. It was as if the windows of heaven were opened and buckets of liquid love were being poured out on me. The glory of the Lord washed over me in wave after wave so much so that I didn't care what people might be thinking of me. I felt literally engulfed in the love of God, and from that day on I have not doubted my salvation.

Some in the church saw the revival as too much emotionalism, but many hearts were changed. I was certainly changed. I was so full of love and joy that I could hardly contain it. I called friends on the phone and wrote letters to others sharing how God had moved in my life. I was aware that God had been with me all my life and how He helped us during Jim's tragic accident, but my new experience was deeply personal. Hunger for the Bible consumed me and I frequented Christian bookstores. On one such occasion I saw a book entitled *They Speak With Other Tongues* by John Sherrill.

Ann and Howard had talked about the gift of speaking in tongues. I wanted to know more. I bought the book. I was completely open to all that God had for me.

Jim and I got quite involved in the Lay Witness Movement. The first mission I found difficult. The coordinators of the mission encouraged us to attend another mission in Oklahoma City, Oklahoma the following month. Reluctantly, we made plans to go.

It was totally different from the first mission. The team was large and included some prominent sports figures. It was exciting and spiritually refreshing. A short time later we were invited to a mission at the First Methodist Church in Tulsa, Oklahoma. Again, the team was exceptional, the testimonies unforgettable and our hostess was wonderful. She was elderly but could not do enough to make us comfortable. The pastor was deeply touched by the Holy Spirit that weekend. When Jim gave his personal testimony he received a standing ovation. Years later, the pastor told us that the mission had a powerful impact on the spiritual life of the church.

Invitations kept coming for us to participate in many other missions all over the country. We found ourselves traveling at least once a month and enjoying the incredible fellowship of dynamic Christians.

One mission brought us to the home of a wealthy business man in Palestine, Texas. After the Saturday night session, the team members were invited to his home for an "after-glow" service. There was singing, fellowship, food, and more testimonies. When the crowd dwindled down to a handful of people, I was in the living room with my hostess while Jim and the men were in another room. My hostess asked me if I had ever heard anyone speak in tongues.

"No, but I read about," I told her. She began praying a beautiful, soft poetic language. The hair on my arms began to rise. I sensed a presence come into the room through the front door and stand right before me. My eyes were closed but I knew it was Jesus. I didn't open my eyes but oh, He was there!

The men called us into the other room and said they would like to pray for Jim and me to receive the Baptism in the Holy Spirit. My hostess was standing by my chair and began speaking softly. I thought she was reading from the Book of Psalms, but when I looked she had no book in her hands.

Jim and I yielded our wills to the will of God that night We both received the baptism in the Holy Spirit and both spoke in tongues. We had been warned that the devil would tell us this was not real. But it was real. God was supplying us with a valuable tool for ministry that was yet to come.

CHAPTER 15

"CALIFORNIA, HERE WE COME"

In Memphis, Jim got involved in CB and Ham radios. I didn't know much about this "hobby", but soon found out it was addictive. Jim kept buying more and better equipment, and spent endless hours talking to strangers. I was glad for him to have something to do since he was confined to the wheelchair, but things were getting out of hand. Jim issued many invitations over the airwaves for people to come visit us. "Y'all come", he said in his southern drawl, and come they did; from the east to the west, from the north to the south, from California to Nova Scotia and points in between. Jim's handle was the "101", named after his airborne unit.

It was not unusual to come home and find a semi-tractor trailer parked on our cul de sac along with several cars. The kitchen would be full of guys sitting around drinking coffee with the very popular "101". An uncle of mine came to visit once and after observing Jim and his obsession with his CB buddies asked me, "How long has he been like this?"

Jim struck up a strong friendship with a group of radio operators in Southern California. When they issued an invitation for our family to visit, Jim expressed interest. I agreed because the McKenneys now lived in Southern California, too. With the Vietnam War raging, Tom had reenlisted in the Marines and was stationed at Camp Pendleton.

We loaded up the station wagon and saw many wonderful attractions on our way to California where we spent the first week with Jim's radio friends. You would have thought Jim was royalty. They had bar-b-ques, get togethers, and fishing trips. Jim enjoyed himself immensely. We met many wonderful people.

When we arrived at the McKenneys the children were thrilled to be together. Tom and Marty had scheduled trips to Disney Land, Knotts Berry Farm, Sea World, and across the border for a day in Mexico. We shared so much fun.

The McKenneys were still good Presbyterians, content in their faith. We had written to them about some of our experiences with the Lay Witness Missions, but stopped short of our encounter with the Holy Spiirit. We figured we would share more with them in person, but somehow the right time didn't come about. We returned home with many happy memories.

Jim called me on the phone one day a few months later to say that he had been asked to participate in a medical convention in Los Angeles. He said I could go as his attendant at government expense. We could take a few extra days and visit the McKenneys in San Diego. I was so excited. Jim's parents were now living in Memphis and would stay with the children. Our plans were shaping up and it was almost time to go when Jim handed me a bombshell! The government would not pay my expenses after all. His attendant must be a government worker. I was crushed. What difference did it make that his wife couldn't be his attendant? I could take better care of him than anybody. Jim was touched by my disappointment and said he supposed we could afford for me to fly separately and go on to San Diego to see our friends. Wow! This was unbelievable….a whole week away by myself. It was more than I could have dreamed of.

Tom and Marty had many things planned for me. Marty took me sightseeing, to lunch and other interesting things. Tom took me, along with their children, on a painting excursion to Laguana Beach, a painter's paradise. The salt air blowing my hair, I sat on huge rocks overlooking the Pacific ocean and painted the sea green water lapping at my feet. It is a memory forever sketched in my mind.

During the entire week I still had not told my friends about my encounter with the Holy Spirit. I wasn't sure how they would react and was still waiting for God to lead me. On my last night there Tom threw the door wide open.

He said, "Ouida, what do you know about the baptism in the Holy Spirit?"

Shocked, I replied, "Well, I believe in it."

Tom leaned forward in his chair and asked, "Why?"

I leaned forward in my chair and said, "Because I have received it." I walked right through the door! I was able to share in great detail all the wonderful things God was doing in our lives. We spent the rest of the evening sharing, and I found out that Tom had encountered some "Jesus People" there in California and was hearing about miraculous things taking place among the hippie population.

God, in his perfect timing, had set up the whole trip. I had a divine appointment in San Diego with the dearest friends we had. God was preparing them spiritually for some rough times ahead. The next time I was to see Tom, he would be a shell of the tough, physically fit Marine I had known.

Shortly thereafter, Tom shipped out to Vietnam and the intense fighting there. As a Lt.. Colonel at the time, he had to give orders he didn't always like, saw killing and dying, and endured the ravages of war under horrible conditions. In a letter he wrote to us from the battle field, he quoted from Romans 8:18, "For I consider that the sufferings of this present time are not worth comparing with the glory that is going to be revealed to us."

Soon afterwards, we received the news that Tom had contracted the tropical intestinal virus known as tropical sprue. Ravaged by the parasites that had invaded his body and unable to retain solid food, he had lost almost half his body weight. His muscles had deteriorated, making it difficult for him to walk. He was sent back to the states for further medical treatment at Walter Reed Hospital.

On his flight to the hospital Tom would be passing through Memphis and decided to stop for a brief visit with us. When I picked him up at the airport, I was saddened to see how much he had aged, how thin he was, and the fact that he leaned heavily on a cane to walk. We discovered that he could eat only baby food and even that gave him terrible stomach cramps. My heart ached because he could not enjoy my cooking he had so relished in the past.

Tom was medically discharged from the US Marine Corps as permanently disabled. He and his family returned to their farm in Kentucky to recoup and regroup. God was not through with the McKenney family though, not by a long shot.

CHAPTER 16

"FINDING MERRYWOOD"

In 1972 Jim accepted a position with the VA Hospital in Gulfport, Mississippi. The offer included the opportunity for him to teach a class on physiatry at the Tulane Medical School in New Orleans. It would be a practical move. We would be closer to Jim's parents, now back in Mobile, and mine.

Jim and I took a trip to the coast to find a house. The Mississippi Gulf Coast had not yet recovered from hurricane Camille, three years earlier. There was still a shortage of available housing, much less wheel-chair accessible homes. We engaged a realtor and were told there was a house in the little town of Pass Christian that might be available so that is where we started looking. It was wheel-chair accessible, but did not meet our needs.

I mentioned to the realtor that I had always wanted to redo an old house on the beach. She informed us that since hurricane Camille there was almost nothing on the beach to buy or rent. She did however, know of an older house on Second Street in "The "Pass" as Pass Christian has always been affectionately called. It was located in the very east end of the town about two blocks from the beach. She took us to see the house and my hopes were dashed. The yard was enough to discourage anyone.

Overgrown weeds and mounds of dirt that had been left over from tree removal almost obscured the old house. The house looked sturdy but was in a terrible state of disrepair.

The backyard was sizable with a large circular cement fountain near the back. Though deep enough to swim in, it was full of debris and algae. A small guest house sat near the back of the yard. It too, needed repairs and was full of junk. Everything needed paint and lots of it. We would not be able to see inside the house until after 5:00 PM when the owner, Mr. Barrett, could bring us a key. I peeked inside the window of the kitchen door and was repulsed by what I saw. Cabinets were in various stages of renovation. Layers of unmatched linoleum were peeling off the floor. From what I could see the kitchen had never been updated. I was not interested in seeing the rest of the house. Besides, and most importantly, it was not wheel-chair accessible.

There were at least five or six steps to every entrance into the house. How in the world would that ever work with a wheelchair? Surely the thirty miles of beachfront property had something more to offer. We decided to look around some more and ended up in Ocean Springs on the east side of Biloxi. I liked what I saw there. One area reminded me of our former neighborhood in Richmond, Virginia. The quaint downtown shops and tree lined streets greatly appealed to me, but not to Jim.

"I want to go back to see the old house in Pass Christian again," he said. It was late afternoon as we found ourselves heading westward. The owner, Mr. Bill Barrett, showed up on time with the key and I was ushered inside. Jim sat in the car and talked to the realtor. The house was filthy dirty; dead roaches littered the floor. The plastered walls were cracked and paint was peeling off the woodwork. The old-fashioned kitchen sink could not be used because the pipes had rusted through. Two adjacent doors in the kitchen led to a partial basement and a secret stairway to the second floor. There was only one very tiny half-bath on the entire main floor. This was the most impractical house for a wheelchair I had ever seen. There was no way I would consider it.

Still......I could see potential. But what was I doing, giving it any serious consideration? Still..... something about the "potential" challenged me. The living-dining room was spacious with a wide fireplace and mantel at one end. There were lots of French door windows. Adjoining the living room was a room that was all windows and French doors. I was told it had once been the music room. But there was no bedroom downstairs. Impossible!

Still... there were four nice bedrooms upstairs and two full-sized bathrooms with the original fixtures, including built-in wooden medicine cabinets and deep slanted-back bathtubs. From the upstairs windows that faced the south you could see the blue waters of the Gulf of Mexico less than half a mile away.

The front porch with its four white round columns and red tile floor was appealing. There was even a screened in back porch with the same red tile floors. Dutch colonial in design, the house had a certain amount of charm, but the staggering repairs and work needed to put it in shape was overwhelming.

I went back outside where Jim was waiting in the car and told him, "The house simply won't work for us, too many barriers, too inconvenient for the wheel-chair."

Jim surprised me by saying, "But I LIKE it. It could be a great place for grandchildren." What could he be thinking? He had not seen the inside, all the work and expense that would be required. As we chatted with the realtor and Mr. Barrett, he told us some interesting things about the house. It had a name, "Merrywood". Merrywood had been built in 1927 for a gentleman named Edward Price Bell, and his wife Mary. Mr. Bell was a famous newspaper journalist who got his start working for the Chicago Daily News. He went on to become the founder of the first foreign news service in London in 1900.

He later became known as America's "Unofficial Ambassador" because of his many interviews of famous people including Adolf Hitler, Benito Mussolini, Pope Pius XI, and many other international leaders. Mr. Bell's office in London became a meeting place for foreign and American dignitaries, since there were no official embassies at the time. He had the distinction to be called by Lord Northcliff (the most powerful newspaper magnate in Britain) "the best American newspaper man London has ever seen." In 1930, Northwestern University proposed Mr. Bell for the Nobel Peace Prize for his years of journalism promoting peace, not war. Upon his retirement, Mr. Bell built Merrywood and a cottage-library behind it where he continued to write and work on his memoirs. He wrapped his property in a fence whose design was reminiscent of the British Union Jack. There he, and his wife Mary, entertained friends and visitors at afternoon teas. Mr. Bell died at Merrywood in 1943.

Mr. Barrett went on to tell us that Merrywood was a virtual showplace in its heyday, surrounded by beautiful landscaping, a reflecting pond with fish and the round fountain that flowed with artesian water. At the present time, the Bell's daughter, Alice Prindeville, was living in her father's library beyond the back yard. It too, needed repairs and painting because of hurricane Camille.

The idea of buying the house was a little more appealing considering its history. Before I finished hearing all the stories Mr. Barrett had to tell me about the house, Jim Tanner was already signing on the dotted line, without ever seeing the inside.

I wanted to set up an appointment to have my parents take a look at the house since my father was knowledgeable about house construction and was an electrician. There were many problems that needed to be addressed and I needed all the help I could get. We made the arrangements and Daddy looked it over carefully, pointing out its good features- its sturdiness, quality of workmanship, the slate "snow" roof, and the fact that it had withstood many hurricanes without structural damage.

He also pointed out the enormous amount of work and expense it would take to make it accessible for the wheelchair. First, we would have to add on a full bathroom on the main floor. A permanent concrete ramp would have to be constructed for wheelchair access to the house. The kitchen needed major updating! What were we thinking? Still........what potential!

Back in Memphis, fears and doubts assailed me. I knew the bulk of the renovations would fall on me. I loved the house we had built in Memphis. It was beautiful and oh, so convenient. We had only lived in it six years- it still smelled new! I didn't want to leave my friends and church either.

Where could I find such good Christian fellowship? Kenny, still in high school, didn't want to leave his friends.

"Lord," I prayed, "If this is really You, then I want to be in the 'nit-ty-gritty' of what You have planned for us. I want to be where the action is, I want to see you move in a mighty way." Wow! Did He ever answer that prayer! Exciting? Yes! An awesome task? Yes! Worth it? In time – yes, yes, yes!

CHAPTER 17

"MOVING TO MERRYWOOD"

July 8, 1972- The moving van pulled into the driveway of 1580 East Second Street, Pass Christian. As I watched the movers take my furniture into the dirty, run-down old house, I already missed my lovely home in Memphis with its many conveniences. The realization of the task before me was overwhelming.

The first thing we had to do was put some long planks on the steps for a make-shift ramp for Jim. With no stove, I had to use portable cooking appliances and had very little counter space on which to put them. The pipes were rusted. I washed dishes in a dish pan and threw the dishwater out the kitchen door. This was worse than our first apartment.

All the family pitched in with the unpacking. Soon, work was going on all over the house: cleaning, painting, installing a permanent ramp for Jim, a new downstairs bathroom, a NEW SINK for the kitchen -- the work never ended.   The yard was screaming for attention but had to wait its turn. No wonder I lost down to 101 pounds that summer.

A few days after we had moved into Merrywood, our next door neighbors paid us a call. They had also moved from Memphis, exactly one year to the day before us. Lewis and Phyllis Levy had much in common with us. Mr. Levy was district manager of Hyster Heavy Equipment Company in New Orleans and commuted to work daily. He also had been involved in CB radio like Jim. Phyllis was an artist. Their son, Lewis had attended Memphis State University, though he and our daughter, Debby, had never met when she was a student there.

The Levys had come bearing a welcome gift - fresh fish from the gulf waters. When they saw how pretty Debby was they wanted their son to meet her. She was getting ready to go to the grocery store for me, and they insisted that she needed someone to drive her. With four vehicles in our driveway, he surely would know it was a set-up. He came anyway, and must have liked what he saw, because from that day on they were a twosome.

The second Sunday we were in Pass Christian, we visited the local Methodist Church. It was small but warm and friendly. We really liked the pastor, Herbert Beasley. He seemed to greatly love the Lord, had a good singing voice and also played guitar. The pianist was nearly ninety years old and was always about four notes behind the singing. She had snow white hair with a gift type bow perched right on top of her head. What a precious soul -- everyone loved her.

We also decided to visit the Methodist church in the next town over, Long Beach. With a vibrant youth ministry, this church better met our family's needs and would be our home church for the next six years. We did remain heavily involved with the Methodist Church in Pass Christian in a life-changing way as well.

I could not believe how quickly we started having house guests. Mostly they came from Memphis, friends of the children. The word had gotten out that the Tanners had bought a big house on the beach. How disappointed they must have been.

Merrywood was far from perfect, and there were many times when I thought we had missed God's leading. I had not yet known about the scripture in Acts 17:26 which says that, "From one man he made every nation of men, that they should inhabit the whole earth; and He determined the times set for them and the exact places where they should live." God was leading.......we were listening.........and trying to learn.

CHAPTER 18

"LIFE BEGINS AT FORTY"

I turned 40 on August 1, 1972. I became a grandmother on August 25th that same year! Talk about a new experience! !

Jason Seth Roach arrived with a head full of thick black hair, a lusty cry and a macho look. It was love at first sight for all of us. Jim and I were so glad that Dawn and Billy had decided to move to Mississippi with us, so that we could be a part of the blessed event. They lived in the guest house for about three months before moving back to Memphis where Billy attended school. Debby started college at the University of Southern Mississippi and Kenny was now the only child at home.

There was still plenty of work to be done at Merrywood and its grounds. But in September the Lord seemed to be saying, "Enough for now. It's time to start your new life." They say that life begins at 40. Indeed, it was a life-changing year for me as I met spiritual mentors and teachers who led me to deeper faith.

I had been neglecting my quiet time with the Lord, using the excuse that I was so very busy. I was physically tired, but even more spiritually tired. I needed the times of refreshing that come from the presence of the Lord. I met a lady from Pass Christian Methodist Church who invited me to attend a Bible study with her in the neighboring town of Bay St. Louis. The Bible study was an outreach of the Trinity Christian Community of New Orleans. commonly called TCC. TCC was a multi-faceted inner city ministry reaching out in love to the homeless, alcoholics, drug addicts, prostitutes, the lonely and unsaved. A Christian coffee house, known as the Upper Room was the starting place. There they were shown love, given food, introduced to Jesus and were taught the Bible. Many of the staff and volunteers were seminary trained and ordained ministers who chose to make this their mission field.

TCC had a well organized plan for new converts. To help them break from their old habits, they were encouraged to move out of the city into a more wholesome environment. A plan was implemented to place these new believers into houses and homes in the small, quiet coastal towns of nearby Mississippi. Houses were purchased or rented for the male converts along with staff members who were mentoring them. The women were placed in private homes of mature Christian families. We were privileged to host one young lady in our home for almost a year. To this very day she still walks closely with the Lord.

One special house in Bay St. Louis, Mississippi, was made into a chapel where worship services and Bible studies were held. Staff members came from New Orleans for weekly studies, which were also open to residents in the area who were interested in the seminary style in-depth studies. I was one such person. When I told God back in Memphis that I wanted to be in the "nitty-gritty" of what He was doing, I did not know what to expect, but somehow I thought this was what I was looking for.

One of the first courses that was taught was "Traina's Inductive Bible Study". The class was fantastic. It was taught by an outstanding seminary professor, Dr. Charles Holman. He was also a gifted violinist, who often blessed us with music. He later received his doctorate degree in Theology from the University of Durham in England and eventually became Dean of Biblical Studies at Regent University in Virginia Beach, Virginia.

His Jamaican born wife, Rosie, was instrumental in the 700 Club prayer ministry at the Christian Broadcasting Network. I mention this to let you know the quality of teachers we were privileged to sit under at the time.

God was preparing us for ministry that was to come later, and He was giving us some of His best instructors.

There were many other great men of God who were involved with the Trinity Christian Community. TCC founder, Rev Bill Brown, had been trained in urban ministry. Dr. George Hays was a Christian counselor and teacher in the New Orleans area. Rev. Mike Barbera, graduate of Princeton Theological Seminary in Princeton, New Jersey, had been moved by the social injustice he saw in urban areas and was eager to work among the lost souls he saw in New Orleans.

Mike met his beautiful southern belle wife there and what a team they made. Together they made wonderful music, ministering in song on many occasions. He later said of his lovely wife, "She's the spice of my life: Sometimes the sugar and sometimes the Louisiana hot sauce." Mike and Margaret Barbera are still some of the most instrumental people in my life. Some years later Mike would become pastor of our church in Pass Christian, Church of the Good Shepherd.

Also, still very influential in my life, are Mike and Sally Cassagne, who graduated from Southeastern Bible College in Lakeland, Florida. They were on staff at TCC and later would also become part of the staff at Church of the Good Shepherd. One never knows what God has in store when He causes people's lives to cross.

There are too many people to mention in the TCC ministry who played major roles in God's plan for our lives and the people of the Mississippi Gulf Coast, but Bill Goheen deserves special recognition. A New Orleans native, Bill was a civil engineer with a major oil company, but resigned his job when he felt the call of God on his life. He became involved with TCC ministry and at the time I met him was working as a dry cleaning delivery man in Bay St. Louis. He was mentoring several of the men who were in the ministry house there. Sweet and gentle of spirit, Bill stood six feet seven inches tall. With my five foot frame I had to crane my neck to look up to him. We were enrolled in some of the same Bible studies.

I heard through the grapevine that Bill needed a place to live. The apartment he was in was only a temporary arrangement. I thought about Merrywood's now empty guest house. At the time, my husband Jim, had not joined me in the bible studies in Bay St. Louis, but he had a growing interest when he realized my enthusiasm over the in-depth studies. I often talked to him about the people I was meeting at the Bible studies. When I told him about Bill Goheen's need for a place to live and mentioned the guest house, he questioned me, "What do you know about this young man?"

As a matter of fact, I knew very little about Bill except that he seemed to be a strong Christian and I liked his spirit. That is what I told Jim and to my surprise he said, "That's good enough for me."

At the next Bible study I went up to Bill and asked him, "Do you need a place to live?"

He looked at me with a big grin and said, "He (meaning Jesus) told you, huh?"

In my wildest dreams I would never have guessed how that one event would affect so many lives in the years to come. It was a God thing all along. He knew how the Merrywood guest house would be used, but if I had known how often it would be used and by whom, I might have had some serious reservations.

About this time I met another lady who would play a very important role in my life. Grace Pfister was an elderly retired school teacher and one of the most godly persons I have ever known. She was a member of the Pass Christian Methodist Church and taught Bible study classes to a group of ladies in the area. She had been a student of the Bible most of her life and probably knew more about the word of God than a lot of ordained preachers. Every Wednesday morning we met in her home, sometimes at church, and did so for nearly thirty years. During that time we covered the Bible from beginning to end, with special emphasis on biblical themes: The Scarlet Thread, The Holy Spirit, Revelations, Major Prophets, Minor Prophets, etc. Sitting around her kitchen table with a cup of coffee I grew in my knowledge of God's Word which helped me immensely as our own ministry opened up.

One of the things that I loved most about Grace was her kindness to others. She never said anything bad about anyone and would not allow others to speak ill of anyone else. She was so full of the Holy Spirit that it reflected in her speech and countenance. Her face literally glowed. She was the perfect example of the older woman spoken of in Titus 2:3-4 where it says that she should teach what is good, and train the younger women to "love their husbands and children, to be self-controlled and pure, to be busy at home...". To me, she personified the woman of Proverbs 31.

Grace also had a green thumb. Everything she put into the ground flourished. Her roses were pure perfection. When I think of Grace I am reminded of Psalm 92: 12-14: "The righteous will flourish like a palm tree, they will grow like a cedar of Lebanon; planted in the house of the Lord, they will flourish in the courts of our God. They will still bear fruit in old age, they will stay fresh and green."

I will be eternally grateful for the blessing of Grace in my life and the lives of so many others. Jim often joined me at Grace's Bible study classes after he retired. It didn't matter to him that he was the only man there. He just loved studying God's Word.

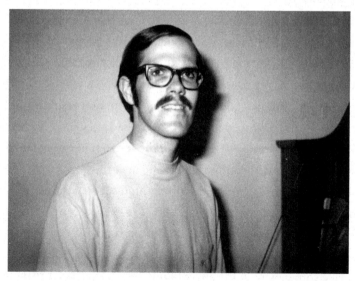

Bill Goheen

CHAPTER 19

"MERRYWOOD MINISTRY"

Bill Goheen moved into the guest cottage two weeks before Christmas. He had his own furniture. A specially ordered king size bed, extra-long to fit his frame, filled the entire small bedroom space. He had a table and two chairs, a chest of drawers and a lamp. He was happy and we were glad to help him out. Bill helped us trim our Christmas tree that year and didn't need a ladder. His size sixteen shoe looked like a boat when I stuck my size four foot into it. Bill was good natured and helpful around the house and yard. He and Jim became great friends. We had no idea of the impact he would have on our lives or that he would be the first of a long list of guests who would occupy the little house over the next thirty-five years

Bill wanted to start a Christian club for high school kids which was part of a national organization called YOUNG LIFE. The Young Life program reached out to teens who might not attend church.. Bill often went to New Orleans during the week to help with the clubs there. He had hoped to find a place somewhere in the area of Long Beach or Pass Christian to start a club on the Mississippi coast. The city limits boundary line between the two towns was one block from our house. God was at work.

Bill invited us to go along with him to one of the Young Life meetings in New Orleans. The session opened with some lively Christian songs. Leaders then played a few funny games with the youth and ended the event with a short Bible study and prayer.

I was impressed at how well behaved the teenagers were and how much they seemed to enjoy having a club of their own. You guessed it! Our home ended up hosting not only the first YOUNG LIFE club on the coast, but the first in the entire of Mississippi! Our son Kenny invited some of his friends. We invited young people from area churches and soon our living room was packed.

Occasionally, Young Lifers would get together with other clubs from Louisiana for joint meetings. These were usually held on Saturdays. Bill asked if we would allow him to invite a group from the Baton Rouge, Louisiana area to come to our house for a meeting. Following the meeting, the youth would spend some time at the nearby beach. It would be a special treat for the them and they would provide their own refreshments as well as clean up afterwards.

Joined with our local club, the group packed the downstairs of our home. Furniture was pushed against the walls to accommodate the musicians and their instruments. As more young people arrived the leaders would tell the already tightly packed ones sitting on the floor, "Tighten up, tighten up!" The kids had a great time and, afterwards they cleaned the grounds so that not a scrap of paper could be found.

Several young guys in our local group, including our son Kenny and some of his close friends, ended up attending a summer Young Life camp in Colorado that year. Many made strong professions of faith to our precious Lord and Savior, Jesus Christ.

To emphasize the effect that the Young Life clubs had in the lives of these teenagers, I share an experience that happened some fifteen or twenty years after the Young Life club met in our home. My doorbell rang at Merrywood, and when I answered there stood a young man I remembered from our former Young Life group. "I can't believe you are still here!" he exclaimed, "You probably don't remember me. I'm....". I quickly interrupted him, "I know who you are, Greg Domert, and I'm delighted to see you." He went on to share with me how his life changed after the Young

Life club. His family had moved away, but Greg had continued his walk with the Lord and was working with the Fellowship of Christian Athletes. He had with him his wife and three little tow-headed boys. What a joy to know! What a wonderful success story! We don't always get to know the results from seeds sown into the kingdom of God.

Bill Goheen continued to be a great spiritual blessing to us during the time he lived in the little guest house. He often attended church with us at the Methodist church in Long Beach. At that time our church did not have a midweek service of any kind. Bill suggested that we have our own Bible study in our house, but not on Wednesday nights because that was the usual night for church mid-week services. We decided that Thursday night would be a better night and would not interfere with other services churches might be having. We chose the book by Watchman Nee entitled *Sit, Walk and Stand* to guide us in our study.

The first night we met there were only four of us....Bill, Jim, Elizabeth Fincher, whom we had met at the Methodist church in the Pass, and myself. She was recently born-again and was hungry for the word of God. After the study we joined together in prayer. It was very simple, very quiet but effective. The date was May 5, 1973. I remembered thinking that it was May 5, 1968 when I was born again in the little Good Shepherd United Methodist Church in Memphis. If someone had asked me if I would like to have a Bible study in my home every Thursday night for twenty-three years, I would have said, "No way!!". But that is what happened over time.

The following Thursday two more ladies joined us, Judy Pucheu and Cheri Mills. Every week new people came. The Lord sent us a great pianist, David Gervais, along with his sister Cathy, who had a beautiful singing voice. We began to have special times of worship before the Bible study. The group always closed in prayer..

By the end of the summer we were having larger crowds. We were not doing anything special to draw them. We just opened our doors and God sent them. They came from different churches, different towns, and occasionally from different states such as Alabama and Louisiana. There were often military people who came from nearby Keesler Air Force base in Biloxi, others from the Seabee Base in Gulfport. A lady once told me," I first heard about your prayer group when we were in Guam."

It was not exactly easy to have anywhere from forty to eighty people in our home at one time. Outside parking was difficult even with our large yard and circular driveway. Seating was also a problem, with folding chairs overflowing into the front foyer, our bedroom, and the back porch. Many people sat on the floor. I had the additional responsibility of making sure the house was clean and light refreshments were served. Some people came straight from work without going home for supper. The least I could do was have fresh coffee, cold fruit punch and cookies. People used to ask me for my punch recipes. I had none. I made it up as I went along from whatever I had in the refrigerator or cupboard. I learned to save juices from canned fruits, and add some ginger-ale or sparkling water to the mix. It was never the same twice.

I had a cleaning lady to come in on Thursdays and really depended on her. Sometimes she could not make it and I would not know until I got home mid-afternoon from driving Jim to New Orleans where he taught at Tulane Medical School. Thursdays were long days for us, but when people started arriving at 7:00 PM we were rejuvenated by their excitement and joy. The hardest part for Jim and me were the late evenings. Some people loved to linger and talk. They did not realize that we had already had a very long day, and the hardest part was yet to come. Jim's personal needs –going to the bathroom, getting a bath and being prepared for bed could take up to two hours. He had to get up at 6:00AM in order to get to work at the Veterans Administration Hospital by 8:00. He depended on me to get him up and off in the mornings. Still, sometimes after Jim had left for work, I would walk across my living room floor and feel the presence of the Holy Spirit lingering in the room. Often I dropped to my knees and thanked Him for what had happened the night before.

One night a young couple visited the prayer group seeking prayer for their infant son. Dr. Dick Caudill and his wife, Patty, had heard about the Thursday night meetings from someone at the Keesler Air Force base where Dick was a dentist. Their son, Benjamin, had been born with a quarter-size hole in his heart. The pediatrician had told the parents that a hole that large was not likely to close by itself and he would probably need surgery. The troubled parents did not want their young son to undergo the surgical procedure and turned to God for answers. They did not bring young Ben to the prayer meeting in our home, but asked only that we pray for him.

Dick and Patty sat side by side in chairs while some of the prayer partners prayed for their son to be healed and for the Holy Spirit to come. After all, it is His power, not ours, that would do the healing work. The next day the Caudills took little Ben back to his doctor, who after examining him over and over, told the parents that the hole in his heart was no longer there. He agreed with them that God had performed a miracle.

With dramatic answer to prayer such as this, more and more hopeful people began showing up at our door on Thursday nights. God was honoring the faithful effectual prayers of people who were in one accord with Him, trying to be obedient to His word. The Bible says in the book of James 5:14, "Is any sick among you? Let him call for the elders of the church to pray over him and anoint him with oil in the name of the Lord. And the prayer offered in faith will make the sick person well; the Lord will raise him up.".

All who came to our fellowship were learning about God's great power and anointing by experience. If God said it in His word, we believed it and that settled it.. That is why we had in depth Bible studies, led by anointed men of God bringing us His word on a weekly basis. We were the only church some people had, even though we emphasized the importance of attending a church regularly and becoming involved members. It was never intended that our prayer group should ever replace or interfere with other churches in the area.

At the time we were still members of the Long Beach Methodist Church. As word of our home group spread, some people in our church attended some of our meetings. We openly discussed our Thursday night meeting with different pastors who served our Methodist Church at the time. Two of our pastors visited our home group in the six years we were members of that church. To our knowledge they did not find our meetings objectionable. We later found out that there were members in the church who had actually discussed asking us to leave the church labeling us "charismatics".

We gave the church members no real reason for wanting us to leave. We were faithful in attendance, gave our tithes and participated in all church related activities. We wanted to be good witnesses to all while not denying Biblical truths that are not always observed by some traditional churches; things like praying for the sick with anointing oil and laying on of hands as found in James chapter 5. We were seeking to be obedient to God's Word as best we could understand it.

CHAPTER 20

"TOUR OF HOMES"

God was moving in so many ways. Life at home was pretty normal. Our oldest daughter, Debby, was finishing her BS degree at the University of Southern Mississippi in Hattiesburg. Dawn, Billy and little Jason were still in Memphis, and our youngest, Kenny was in high school in Pass Christian. He was becoming more content as he made new friends. Work was still going on at Merrywood, though it seemed we would never finish.

We were asked by the city to participate in the annual Tour of Homes. While I didn't feel we were ready for such a thing, they talked us into it. Some of our prayer group friends helped us spruce up the place, including the yard. It was spring-time and it seemed that God made everything bloom at just the right time; the azaleas, wisteria, dogwoods, etc. put on a fine show. The large round fountain in the backyard had been repaired and now had fresh running water, making a lovely splashing sound as it cascaded over the center pedestal. I had asked the prayer group to pray that people would feel the Holy Spirit throughout the house and yard. We prayed over everything and some of the ladies volunteered to be tour guides. I was pretty nervous, especially when I realized that a whole bus load of interior decorators from New Orleans would be coming to see the place.

My fears were unfounded as I heard remarks like, "they saved the best for last." Others were heard saying, "There's something about this place. I don't want to leave." One lady came back through the house a second time because she liked the spirit of the place. It was the prayer that had been offered up prior to the tour and God deserves the glory.

It so happened that an unusual event transpired at the same time as our house tour. The Chicago Daily News newspaper where Edward Price Bell got his start in journalism was going out of business. Mr. Bell's daughter, Alice Bell Prindeville, was still living in her father's library behind Merrywood and was interviewed by the local newspaper about her father's involvement with the Chicago Daily News. Our local paper carried a full page article on Mr. Bell's library and his years as a journalist. There were interesting comments about Merrywood, including a picture of its 15 degree pitch snow roof. Also included was the fact that Merrywood would be on the Tour of Homes. Interest was high..

God continued to surprise us with unusual things about the old house named Merrywood, a house that seemed to have a personality of its own.

CHAPTER 21

"MILITARY MINISTRY"

While Jim and I were attending a Friday night service at the First Methodist Church in Pass Christian, I noticed a nice looking young man sitting alone on the back row. He appeared to be in his early twenties and looked lonely. I felt the Lord would have me befriend him. His name was Randy Graham and he was a II Lieutenant stationed at nearby Keesler Air Force Base in Biloxi. I invited Randy to our home for coffee and refreshments after the service, which he accepted. Over refreshments we realized that he was searching for answers concerning his faith, or lack thereof. Jim and I shared some of our experiences and he seemed eager to know more.

It had been a long day for Jim. I excused myself and helped him to bed. I returned to the living room, Bible in hand, where Randy had question after question. He seemed particularly concerned about some of his acquaintances and how to witness to them. He had not yet read the Bible and was not knowledgeable of the scriptures.

I opened my Bible to I Corinthians 1:18. "For the message of the cross is foolishness to those who are perishing. But to those who are being saved it is the power of God." I also shared how important it is to have the Holy

Spirit in our lives, because it is He who gives us the boldness and the power to witness about Jesus. I pointed out I Corinthians 2:14 that says, "The man without the Spirit does not accept the things that come from God, for they are foolishness to him and he cannot understand them because they are spiritually discerned."

We talked and talked. It was getting quite late and I invited Randy to stay the night in one of the upstairs bedrooms if he liked. He accepted the offer, but after I had gone to bed I heard him come downstairs and leave the house. I figured he didn't like what I had shared with him or else the devil told him it was all a lie. I said a prayer for him. rolled over and went to sleep.

Very early the next morning I heard voices coming from the living room. Slipping on my robe, I found Randy and a friend sitting on the living room sofa. His friend was his roommate who shared his condo. Randy had rudely awakened him at 3:00 AM excitedly telling him about his experience at our house.

Jim and I gave Randy a copy of *The Way*, a modern translation of the Bible, and he was devouring it. Soon after, he received the baptism of the Holy Spirit through another group of believers, with the evidence of speaking in tongues. Randy was on fire!

One Sunday night Randy joined us for services at Long Beach Methodist Church. Gray-haired Rev. Waugh suggested that we sing the old spiritual hymn, "The Pentecostal Power". You could feel the spirit! Then we sang "Let the Redeemed of the Lord Say So". Rev. Waugh then did an unusual thing. He invited anyone who had experienced something special from the Lord in the past week to stand up and testify, A lady stood up and said, "My daughter had a large growth on her arm and after prayer at the Tanner's house, it just fell off!" Her daughter lifted her healed arm as evidence.

Slowly, others began sharing how God had touched their lives in some way. And then Randy stood up. So did the hair on my arms. My heart was racing and I didn't know what to expect next. Randy's face turned red and out of his mouth poured forth the most fluent unknown language I had ever heard. I immediately understood it was the Holy Spirit speaking through him, but many did not know or understand. For the edification of the church though, God gave Carolyn Lero, who was a church member and also moved in the gifts of the Spirit, the beautiful interpretation.

I have come to realize that God has his own timing to introduce the mysteries of his supernatural power to whomever and wherever he chooses. The vessel he chose that night was a brand-new, on-fire Christian named Randy Graham.

I was present when Randy got baptized. He had become friends with a black pastor in Biloxi, Brother Nichols, and that's who baptized him. It took place just north of Gulfport, along the banks of rural Red Creek. It was a warm morning and a large crowd of people was there. Several baptisms were taking place, Homemade stalls had been set up for dressing rooms along the sandy bank. The women were mostly dressed in white. Randy wore overalls. It was so moving; like a beautiful, primitive painting.

There was spontaneous singing of old spiritual songs and a lot of "hallelujahs!" When Randy came up out of the water his face was absolutely radiant. He was grinning ear to ear and his hands were raised high in praise to God. What a glorious occasion and I am so glad I got to be a part of it.

There are many more Randy stores I could relate, but space does not permit. We were sorry when Randy was discharged from the military and left the area. We lost touch for a while but I am happy to say that today he is happily married, has four children and is still actively serving the Lord. I was especially touched to know that he and his wife have a little guest house in their backyard and often host missionaries and other Christians in need of lodging. When Randy told me that it was our hospitality that had inspired them to do that, I was deeply humbled.

I love Hebrews 13:2 which says, "Do not forget to entertain strangers, for by so doing some people have entertained angels without knowing it." Imagine the honor of entertaining angels!

Many other young military guys began showing up at our Thursday night prayer meetings. Some from Keesler, some from the Seabee base, some from the Coast Guard. I don't know how they found out about our home group but we were delighted to have them. Sometimes they would ask if they could come visit us on Saturdays when they were free. They wanted to sit at Dr. Tanner's feet and have him teach the Bible to them.

Occasionally, I would cook for them. One particular Saturday I had planned to cook shrimp for them, but when I saw such a large group I was worried that I would not have enough for all. I recalled how Jesus fed the five thousand with five loaves and two fishes, so I prayed and asked God to multiply the shrimp.. Did He ever! I cooked and cooked until the platter was overflowing and still we had shrimp left over. This time the lesson was for me.

CHAPTER 22

"THE HOLY SPIRIT CONFERENCES"

The Pass Christian Methodist Church continued to play a significant role in our spiritual growth. Because we met a lot of people who attended the TCC Bible studies there, one couple in particular became some of our dearest friends, Bob and Marge Jones. Bob was a plumber and his wife helped her parents run a dry cleaning business. They were our age and we spent a lot of time in fellowship together. They also regularly attended our Thursday night prayer group.

Bob shared with Jim how he felt the call of God on his life to become an ordained minister of the gospel. Jim encouraged him and at middle age Bob sold his plumbing business, enrolled in the Baptist Seminary in New Orleans and became an ordained Methodist minister in Mississippi where he remains today.

The Pass Methodist Church invited guest speakers from time to time. It was there that we met Rev. Andy Gallman, and Rev. Bertist Rouse, both serving as full-time evangelists for the United Methodist Evangelistic Association. We became good friends and invited them to speak at our Thursday night prayer meetings. They expressed an interest in sponsoring a conference on the Holy Spirit on the Gulf Coast. As plans evolved, Jim was appointed co-chairman of the conference, along with Bill Frith, a dear brother in Christ. Since both Jim and Bill had full-time jobs, the bulk of the leg-work fell on me. I quickly realized how much preparatory work went into such an event.

That first conference was such a success that annual Holy Spirit conferences were established, running for the next ten years. During that time we had an array of outstanding speakers, including Jack Gray, Robert Coleman, Father Barham, Jamie Buckingham, Mark Rutland, Bob and Ellen Degroon Stamps, Dr. Bob Wise, Dr. Bill Thomas (pastor of Tulsa First Methodist), Bob Shelley,, Vicki Jameson, Jimmy Buskirk, Bishop Stokes of the Methodist Seashore District, and many others. It was wonderful to hear these outstanding men of God speak about the Holy Spirit. For us personally, it was thrilling to get to know some of these giants of the faith as we broke bread together and shared quiet talks

We were especially grateful for the opportunity to host Bob and Ellen Degroon Stamps and their son, Peter John, for an overnight visit at Merrywood. Ellen had been Corrie Ten Boom's traveling companion for more than ten years. When Corrie Ten Boom and Ellen visited the United States they always stopped first at the home of Dr. Mike and Fran Ewing in Florida. The Ewings had come to the Holy Spirit conference to see them. Dr. Ewing and Dr. Tanner had a lot in common. Both were in wheelchairs and both had medical degrees in the special field of Physical Medicine and Rehabilitation.

Bob and Ellen gratefully accepted our invitation to stay overnight and to indulge in a lavish seafood dinner at Merrywood. It was Sunday afternoon and, with the conference over; a time to relax, rest and let our hair down. Bob took a liking to Merrywood. He walked around the house, touching the woodwork and made a comment I shall never forget. "Don't ever sell this house, don't ever sell this house". Those words would haunt me many years later when circumstances dictated that we would have to make a major decision concerning the grand old house.

I have fond memories of that afternoon. Our black and white shepherd mix dog had just had a litter of healthy, plump and fuzzy puppies, much to the delight of Peter John. Over dinner Jim happened to share how we had participated in the Bible studies through TCC. We mentioned that our friend, Dr. Charles Holman, was working on his Doctorate in Biblical Studies at the University of Durham in England. Bob's ears perked up and he wanted to know more about Dr. Holman. Oral Roberts University was losing its professor of Biblical studies to Regent University in Virginia Beach. They were searching for someone to replace him and Bob liked what we were sharing about Charles.

Bob asked if he could use our phone to place a call to Dr. Holman in England. We were happy to oblige and things were set in motion to have Charles fly to Tulsa for an interview in the near future. As it turned out, ORU had to put a moratorium on hiring at the time and would not be able to have Charles come on staff. However, through the divine providence of our Lord, he was offered a position at Regent University which he accepted and remained there until his death from cancer many years later. He was much revered by the staff and students alike. CBN founder, Pat Robertson gave the eulogy at Charles' memorial service. His wife, Rosie, remained deeply involved with CBN's telephone prayer ministry. I am continually amazed at how God brings people together to accomplish his will.

CHAPTER 23

"WALKING IN THE SPIRIT"

The Holy Spirit was being poured out in great measure along the Mississippi Gulf Coast in the 70's and early 80's. We were eager to be a part of this move and had witnessed supernatural manifestations of the gifts of Holy Spirit in our own home meetings. We felt called to find a more charismatic home church.

We found that home in New Covenant Church. It was a new church co-pastored by two good friends of ours. Howard Beam, an ordained Baptist preacher, and Ray Powers, an ordained Assembly of God preacher, were of different denominational backgrounds but one in spirit and vision. Another church was providing space for New Covenant to meet on Sunday afternoons, but the church needed an office of its own during this start up and organizational period. So once again the Tanner's guest cottage came to the rescue. For over a year there were no guests in the guest house. The church started growing.

The Thursday night meetings continued to grow as well. The music at our prayer meetings was heavenly, healing the spirit. It didn't matter if we had a pianist or not. It became a tradition to open the meeting with a song with the words, "I don't know what you came to do but I just came to praise the Lord." And our favorite, "We have come into this house to magnify His name and worship Him". We often sang a lilting chorus, "I want to testify, I want to tell, what the Lord has done for me." During this song people would stand up and give what we called "Popcorn" testimonies of what the Lord had recently done for them. It was encouraging and faith building.to hear how God was moving in lives.

Jim and I along with our good friends, Bill and Penny Frith, often went to services and revivals in other churches. One evening as we were preparing to go to a Baptist church in Gulfport, I was trying to put the final touches on my hair-do while the others were waiting for me in the van. It was a rainy, blustery evening so I figured I had better go heavy on the hair-spray. With my eyes closed I picked up the can of spray and pushed the button. Gee, that smells awful funny and it sure is drippy wet I thought to myself. I opened my eyes to see a head that looked like sheep skin on top. I had sprayed my hair with Lysol Foaming Bathroom Cleaner! What a mess and the car horn kept honking. I took a towel and blotted, then the hair dryer and did my best to redeem the do, but I couldn't get rid of the odor. A heavy spray of perfume ought to do it. Wrong! I just hoped I wouldn't have too many "holy hugs" that night. It reminded me of the time that I brushed my teeth with "Icy Hot" just before a service I was attending. And I was the speaker!

Jim and I had both been baptized in Methodist churches, but felt that we now wanted to be baptized in the same manner as our Lord. When a group of local Christians were being baptized in the nearby Wolf River, we decided to make sure we were properly immersed, and besides it would be more meaningful this time. We wondered how it would work since Jim couldn't walk down the river bank and out on the white sand-bar. Several of his friends carried him down, sat him in the shallow water and the preacher laid him back until he was properly dunked. It was a memorable occasion.

As you might expect, everybody that knew us wanted to see Jim Tanner healed of his paralysis. Nobody wanted it more than I did and I had prayed every day for all the long years he had been in the wheelchair. We went to healing services where he was anointed with oil and prayed over by many pastors and laymen. There were times when men would get on each side of Jim, holding him up and trying to get him to take a step. He would try so hard, but his legs just crumpled under him. What bothered him the most was when someone would say to him, "Brother, you just don't have enough faith." That hurt. I knew what a great man of faith my husband was, and I had heard him pray, "I believe, Lord, help my unbelief."

During this period Kathryn Kuhlman, a well-known faith healer, was holding a crusade in Mobile, Alabama. We made plans to go, along with a large group of strong prayer warriors from our prayer group. The atmosphere was electric. Jim's folks lived in Mobile and we had invited them to go. Our son Kenny went too, but chose to sit alone in the top row of the large coliseum.

I looked around the huge auditorium; some faces hopeful, some crying, many on stretchers, hundreds in wheelchairs, many deformities, some obviously dying cancer patients; what a sad mass of humanity. I looked at Jim, neatly dressed and sitting upright in his wheelchair, an over-comer in so many ways; a professional man, a beloved doctor, a happy countenance surrounding him. The organist was playing "It Is Well With My Soul". I looked at Jim and he was shining with the love of God. Those who had come with us were disappointed that Jim wasn't physically healed, but when they looked down on him from the balcony, they saw his radiance and knew all was well with his soul.

Kenny stayed in his seat on the top back row and didn't come down until we left. He is a strong Christian now and understands that God has his own plans for people's lives, but at that time his faith was shaken.

CHAPTER 24

"MCKENNEYS IN MINISTRY"

After his medical discharge from the Marines, Tom McKenney and family settled in Kentucky. There, Tom immersed himself in studying the Bible and was becoming quite the Biblical scholar. He still suffered from the effects of the tropical sprue he had contracted in Vietnam, moving slowly with a cane, but growing a bit stronger.

The family came to see us at Merrywood often. It saddened me that Tom could no longer eat my cooking, which he loved. He tried but his digestive system would still only tolerate bland foods.

On one visit, Bill Goheen asked us to attend a Lay Witness Mission in a nearby town in Louisiana where Tom received prayer for healing. Imagine my joy when two days later I heard a commotion in the living room. There was Tom McKenney—minus the cane—pushing Jim and his wheelchair in circles. Both were singing and praising the Lord. Later when Tom found and ate a piece of leftover fried chicken without consequences, we knew the healing was complete!

Tom had been a gung-ho marine and now he was a gung-ho spirit-filled Christian. He often taught the Bible to our Thursday night group and was so popular that locals wanted him to teach on a regular schedule.

There was the distance of some 700 miles between our homes, which made scheduling difficult. However, air fares were much cheaper in those days and he could fly round trip for about $65. Thus began a period of monthly teachings by Tom to everyone's delight.

Tom's reputation as a Bible teacher had begun to spread which put him in demand in areas near his home in Kentucky and Tennessee, as well as the Mississippi Gulf Coast. In time, Tom founded "Words for Living Ministries". It includes monthly newsletters, speaking and teaching engagements, a book ministry, Christian retreats, foreign missions and eventually included working with veterans affairs- especially those involving prisoners of war.

We were thrilled when the McKenneys decided to buy a home on the coast, where several of their children also elected to live. Their son, Jeff, became a medical missionary and founded a hospital in Honduras called Loma de Luz, which means "light on a hill". Dr. McKenney literally brought medical facilities into an area where there were no roads, no water or electricity The Cornerstone Foundation was established in 1992 by Dr. Jeff McKenney and its office is based in D'Iberville, Mississippi. The non-profit hospital is serving not only the physical needs of the Hondurans, but also the spiritual needs. The ever-expanding ministry now includes schooling for children, lodging for patients' families and housing for full time staff.

What a joy it has been through the years to see what God has done in and through this remarkable family and how privileged we have been to have shared their friendship over the years. The McKenneys and the Tanners have many mutual friends and often have found our lives intertwined.

One such couple was Bill and Sue Waters. Bill was a captain in the Navy Seabees and the commander of the base in Gulfport when we first met. They often attended our Thursday night meetings. Bill was soon afterwards appointed the commander of the Camp David facilities in Maryland, outside Washington, D.C. It was his duty to prepare and secure Camp David for all activities there, including presidential visits, government officials, and foreign dignitaries' meetings. At that particular time President Ronald Reagan was in office. When he was at Camp David, Captain Waters rarely left his side.

The Waters family was allowed to have visits from friends and family on the premises in their private quarters as long as there were no official governmental activities taking place at the same time. It so happened that Tom McKenney was going to be in Quantico, Virginia about the same time as Jim and I were in the area on a vacation. Bill Waters invited us all to visit with him and Sue as there were no governmental functions scheduled at Camp David on that particular weekend.

We could hardly believe this was happening to us. After all, how many people ever get to set foot on Camp David much less spend a weekend? We had to be cleared by the Secret Service, or course, which was handled by our friend, Bill. It felt strange being searched and having our vehicle searched with mirrors before entering the grounds. Captain Waters gave us the grand tour. The Camp David facilities were rustic and relaxing, the fall leaves were constantly being blown off the roadways in the event of an unexpected presidential arrival.

It all seemed surreal- being in such an important place, where so many famous world leaders often spent many hours in diplomatic relations. We had a wonderful time reminiscing and talking about the Lord, with breakfasts on the patio and dinners in the Waters' modest home. What are the chances of something like this happening between friends who were from different walks of life, lived in different states , and just happened to be in this special place, at this appointed time? There is only one answer: it was a God thing. God was the common denominator in our knowing each other in the first place. Only He could have made the connections!

On a more personal note, I remember an incident when Tom was visiting us at Merrywood. I awoke one morning quite early to the aroma of coffee brewing and went into the kitchen to find Tom sitting at the kitchen table. His face was wet with tears. "What on earth is the matter?" I inquired of him. "I don't know, Ouida. I went for an early morning walk on the beach and suddenly was just overcome with the need to cry. I have no idea what I am crying about."

But I knew. The very night before I had read a teaching on the subject of our tears; how important they are to God, and how they often cleanse the soul. It dealt with our tears as expressed in Psalm 56:8, (KJV). "Put thou my tears in thy bottle. Are they not numbered in your book?" God sees , knows, and records in writing all our trials, sufferings, pain and yes, tears. Every tear we shed is carefully preserved in His memory.

Jesus, Himself, shed tears. He wept over Jerusalem before He entered the city before His crucifixion. He wept over the death of his friend, Lazarus, and the grief of his sisters, Mary and Martha. But He never wept for himself. He assures us in Revelation 21:4 that there will be no tears in heaven. "God will wipe away every tear from their eyes."

Why was Tom crying that morning? God was preparing him to write a wonderful teaching on "Precious Are the Tears" which would minister to countless people in the years ahead.

CHAPTER 25

"ALL WE LIKE SHEEP"

I love Passover! But when we first moved to the coast I knew very little about the celebration of Passover. I'm sure I had read about it in the Old Testament but like so much of my earlier years of reading the Bible I had simply passed over its deep spiritual meaning. When my friend Carolyn Lero approached me about having a Passover celebration at one of our meetings, I didn't know where to start. She had participated in Passover in a former church so I counted on her to take the helm in making the plans. We were to keep it simple- using the symbolic foods and keeping the emphasis on Passover being the forerunner of our Christian institution of Holy Communion.

We set up long tables in our living/dining area, covered them with white cloths and decorated them with flowers and candles. On small white plates we laid out the symbolic foods; unleavened bread or matzo, charoseth (a mixture of apples, cinnamon, and nuts representing brick mortar), horse-radish for bitter herbs, a small cup of salt water, and a small goblet of grape juice for wine. Several hymns were sung and then the story of the original Passover was read from Exodus 12. Recounting the Israelites' delivery from their years of bondage in Egypt, the chapter describes in detail how the blood of an innocent lamb marking the doorpost would cause the angel of death to pass over the home. This clearly foretold how the blood of the sinless Jesus would mark a wooden cross to deliver us from the bondage of sin.

I have participated in many Passovers over the years, some with Jews for Jesus, some with dramas and full course meals, some simply sharing symbolic foods, but always, with renewed gratitude that the Jewish people have kept this important celebration in observance of the great story in Exodus.

Once I was invited to speak at a Women's Aglow luncheon in Vicksburg, Mississippi. It was held at the Ramada Inn on the banks of the majestic Mississippi river. Since it was nearing the Easter season, I felt impressed to speak on the meaning of Passover and how Jesus is truly our Passover Lamb. The gospel is meant to be understood. No clearer illustration of the love of God for his children can be seen than that of a shepherd caring for his sheep.

I used Phillip Keller's book *A Shepherd Looks At The Good Shepherd And His Sheep* as my guide. I learned that sheep have need of a shepherd. More than any other livestock they require attention and meticulous care. A good shepherd builds a sheep-fold to protect his sheep at night from predators and weather. It is similar to a barnyard or a pasture with a fence around it, with a gate where the sheep enter in. The good shepherd leads the sheep out early in the morning while dew is still on the ground. He finds green pastures and fresh water for them. He gains their trust by speaking kindly to them and caressing them.

The shepherd's voice plays a vital role in the relationship between sheep and their shepherd. Over a period of time sheep come to know that the sound of the shepherd's voice brings them benefits. Oh, that we humans could learn to trust our Good Shepherd's voice like that. When sheep recognize their shepherd's voice, they will respond at once. Even if they are fighting they will stop, cock their heads and run toward the shepherd. But to a stranger's voice they will not respond. How important it is for us to know the Master's voice only, and not listen to false shepherds.

Sheep cannot be driven, they must be led. That is why sometimes a shepherd will pick up a little lamb and carry it in his arms. He knows the mother ewe will be sure to follow.(John10:5) Sometimes a sheep will willfully pull away from following, and the shepherd has to take his staff and pull him back into the fold. The staff has many purposes. Its crook can lift a lamb from a dangerous spot. It is also useful for the shepherd to lean on when he is tired. "Thy rod and thy staff, they comfort me." (Psalm 23:4) The sheep are checked each day by their shepherd for cuts and bruises. He anoints their heads with oil to keep away parasites.. Sheep will not lie down for four reasons: (1)if they are afraid (2) if they are mad at other sheep (3) if they are tormented by flies or parasites (4) if they are hungry. Can you relate?

Sheep will blindly, habitually, stupidly follow one another along same little trails until they go over a cliff or fall into a ravine. So it is with people. "All we like sheep have gone astray." (Isaiah 53:6). Sheep are easily panicked, but can sometimes stand still and stare blankly when a predator comes among them. If a sheep falls over on its back with his feet up, gasses begin to build up and expand in the rumen. If the shepherd does not come to help him, he will die. That is why a shepherd counts his sheep often to see if one is missing. If one is missing, time is of the essence. The shepherd breaks into a run, leaving the others behind in order to rescue the lost sheep. Jesus compares us to sheep in Mathew 18:12-14.

Does this not bring to mind words of songs and hymns, scriptures and parables of Jesus? Can you not see that Jesus, the Lamb of God, is also the Good Shepherd?

When I had finished my talk on sheep, I did a large colored chalk drawing of Jesus on the cross, with a father and two sons standing nearby. They had come to Jerusalem to bring a little lamb for Passover, and got caught up in the crucifixion crowd. The very popular song of that day, "Watch the Lamb" played in the background as I finished the picture.

Afterwards as we sat at lunch, a gentleman across the table from us spoke up and said, "Those things you said about sheep are true. I know, I'm a shepherd." He had my attention.

"Oh, you mean you are a pastor?" I asked.

"No, I am a shepherd. I raise sheep across the Mississippi river in east Louisiana."

I sat in stunned silence. What were the chances of meeting a real live shepherd in the Ramada Inn in Vicksburg, Mississippi! He was an advisor to that particular Women's Aglow chapter. But his presence there was also for me, confirming that I had indeed heard from my Good Shepherd in bringing the appropriate message for that day.

CHAPTER 26

"Y'ALL COME"

There's nothing like the beautiful Mississippi Gulf Coast. White sandy beaches, southern hospitality, fresh seafood, and New Orleans is only an hour away! "Y'all come on down. This is the 101 signing off."

Not again! Our son-in-law, Lewis, had given Jim his father's Ham radio equipment after his dad's death. In all fairness to Lewis, he did approach me with the idea realizing that I might not be entirely favorable after the problems we'd had in Memphis. I was torn. I knew Jim had really enjoyed talking to other CBers around the country. It was top of the line equipment. Jim would love that! Still...

My main objection to having him get involved in this hobby again was his generous invitation to have all his radio buddies come visit him in our home. I remembered only too well all those days of strangers crisscrossing the country to visit the "101" back in Memphis. Jim would have to promise on a stack of Bibles that he would not issue open invitations to people all over the world to visit Merrywood. He promised.

I wanted to believe him. He was so happy with all that fancy equipment that now helped him reach farther and farther away. But, just as I had expected, I overheard him talking to a guy in Tasmania and inviting him to come visit us in Mississippi. "Don't worry, Ouida, no one is going to come all the way from Tasmania." But guess what? The first ones to come were from Tasmania, a family of four. Very nice and interesting people, but weren't they all? My problem was how to entertain them for a week, what to feed them . Jim had a full time job so the bulk of the "hosting" fell on me.

And thus began another lengthy parade of radio friends, this time most of them were from foreign countries; Australia, New Zealand, England as well as California and points west. And they ALL wanted to visit New Orleans. I became a regular tour guide.

How was I doing with the Bible's admonition to "Practice hospitality to one another without grumbling?" (I Peter 4:8) I was struggling. I had never intentionally been inhospitable to any guests, no matter how inconvenient. It was not their fault that they had been graciously invited into our home. But I was physically and emotionally drained. Added to the daily routine of caring for a paraplegic husband and the weekly prayer meetings in our home, what was I to do?

I longed for the day when Jim would realize that this could not continue. Finally he too, was worn out. He sold the equipment, and replaced it with a computer and discovered Christian chat rooms. We only had one internet guest visit. Following an extended stay from a middle-aged woman who envisioned our little guest house as the perfect place to live while she set up a T-shirt business on the coast, I laid down the law! The computer could stay, but chatting was forbidden..

It seemed that when the Lord showed us who should stay in the guesthouse, things worked out fine. If someone else asked us to keep people for a given time there were often problems. We were asked to let a young married couple stay in the little house for a week, which turned into eleven weeks. They took advantage of our hospitality, spending most of their time in our house, eating our food and controlling our TV. They were indignant when we asked them to leave. Other "visitors" trashed the place, left spoiled food in the fridge and wet towels on the floor.

For the most part, over the years and the hundreds, (literally) of people who stayed there, the folks were very appreciative and a joy to have. I am truly thankful that we were able to help lots of people when they were in transition or just needed a place to pray, write a book, or have a respite of peace.

Meanwhile, back at the big house, life was always busy. We met some of the most wonderful people in the world during our Thursday night meetings and through traveling Christians who needed overnight lodging. Christ for the Nations buses were often parked in our driveway. Jews for Jesus made regular stops on their travels along Interstate 10. We really were on the beaten path.

I loved it when we got to host the African Children's Choir. They were the sweetest, most lovable children. They called us mama and poppa. Volunteers from up north came down to New Orleans for Mardi Gras ministry every year and needed a place to stay.

New Life for Girls must be mentioned. Based in Pennsylvania, this ministry to wayward girls was patterned after David Wilkerson's ministry Teen Challenge. New Life had set up homes in several states in order to reach more girls. Pass Christian had been selected to have a host home for them. Located in a rural area away from shopping centers and other distractions, the girls were taught the Bible, how to live the Christian life and in general start a new life. We became active in their ministry and Jim was on the board of directors. He also served in the capacity of family physician to them. I taught classes in personal grooming, etiquette, and home-making.

Sometimes the counselors needed a break and would come spend a day or two at Merrywood. One dear saint we met through the ministry was Sister Kathleen Spurlin, a Catholic nun who had shed her habit for conservative regular dress. She often attended our prayer group and was active in jail ministry. Later she became the first female prison chaplain to the South Mississippi Regional Prison Facility in Leakesville, Mississippi, the same town we had lived in when Jim was injured. It was a new facility and we would become involved in that ministry over time.

CHAPTER 27

"GUESTS AT MERRYWOOD"

Meanwhile, back at Merrywood, we had some very special folks living with us. Our dear friends, Rev. Mike and Margaret Barbera of TCC days needed a temporary home because he was between church pastorates. Mike and Margaret and their infant daughter, Melody, lived with us for thirteen months.

We enjoyed having the Barberas in our home. Margaret was excellent help in the kitchen; Mike too, for that matter. He made delicious Italian dishes and was helpful around the house and grounds. Mike wanted to contribute financially toward their room and board. We did not expect or want any remuneration. He served us in so many ways.

The Barberas had a few financial obligations of their own, however, like a car note and insurance. To see God constantly meet their needs was a faith building experience. Mike took odd jobs, even unloading bananas and heavy bags of grain at the port in Gulfport. As he worked , Mike sought opportunities to reach the lost for Jesus. Perhaps one day he will know just how many of those seeds sown among dock workers grew to fruition .

Mike was also asked to speak at various churches, Full Gospel Business Men's groups, etc. He frequently taught the Bible studies in our home group. Often envelopes arrived in the mail with just the right amount of money to meet his family's needs. God did open the door for Mike to pastor a church in Dyersburg, Tennessee. But God was not done with the Barberas and their relationship with the Tanners, and the folks on the Mississippi Gulf Coast. Years later he would return to the coast to pastor The Church of the Good Shepherd.

We had other long-term guests at Merrywood. Sharlene Rouse, daughter of Rev. Bertist and Anna Merle Rouse lived with us while attending Gulf Coast Jr. College in Biloxi. Mike Ramsey, the son of dear friends, was with us for a period of nearly three years as he finished college while his parents were overseas with the military in Japan. We had the privilege of hosting the children of missionary evangelist David Saint of Argentina, Billy and Damaris, while they attended the English school at University of Southern Mississippi In Hattiesburg.

We had met the incredibly wonderful Saint family through our association with Tom McKenney. Phil Saint was an evangelist who had the amazing gift of illustrating his sermons with colored chalk drawings. Phil's own father, Lawrence, a stained glass artist , made the beautiful Rose Window in the National Cathedral in Washington, D.C. Phil's brother, Nate was the pilot who along with Jim Elliott and others, were killed by the Auca Indians in the jungles of Ecuador in the mid 1950's. Their sister, Rachel had gone back into the jungles along with Elizabeth Elliott and spent the rest of her life evangelizing the savages who had massacred the missionaries.

Native witnesses to the event later told Rachel an amazing story. On the opposite side of the river that fateful day, a large group of indigenous people had witnessed the massacre. They were terrified as the sky above the dying missionaries filled with a heavenly host of angels in white garments and blowing golden trumpets welcomed the martyrs to their heavenly homes. These people who had once fled in fear now rejoiced that their names too were written in the Lamb's Book of Life.

Phil Saint and his family moved to Argentina and began a ministry there. Phil and his wife, Ruth, made frequent trips to the U.S. to visit churches that helped support their ministry. Everywhere they went Phil preached and drew his beautiful pictures. We invited Phil and Ruth to stay in our home during their travels in the states. What a blessing they were. Their sweet spirits refreshed us and they were refreshed by our hospitality. I loved to spoil them, bringing them hot tea by the fireplace and helping Phil set up his easels when he spoke in local churches. I watched him paint many beautiful scenes over the years but none moved me so much as his drawing of the "Palm Beach" story depicting the yellow plane on a river bank and the missionaries martyred there.

Phil often painted pictures for our Thursday night meetings. How blessed we were by his true stories so vividly brought to life in his illustrations. The last time Phil was in our home he asked me to help him with a book he was writing. We spread papers all over our dining room table, sorting the chapters and making notes. I was so honored to be asked to help.

Ruth was not with him on that last trip. They were to celebrate their 50th wedding anniversary as soon as he got back to Argentina. Our last letter from Phil talked about how wonderful the occasion had been. Soon afterwards we received the tragic news that Phil had been killed in an accident. He had been grading a steep road on their property when the dirt gave way causing Phil and the tractor to plummet down the mountainside. His hat had fallen off in the road and that is how he was found.

The news broke my heart. I wept and wept over this dear old saint, who was so aptly named Saint. The last thing he had done before he went out on the tractor that day was to sign his name to a large painting that he had done of the "Palm Beach" martyr story, this time with a new addition. He had depicted the heavenly host above the scene welcoming the saints home.

I have a copy of that painting and it is indeed awe inspiring. Later I felt impressed to do a portrait of Phil in front of a portion of that painting. It now hangs in the Conference Center in Argentina.

CHAPTER 28

"THE WURMBRAND'S VISIT"

O f all the guests we hosted in the little cottage, none is more memorable than that of Pastor Richard Wurmbrand and his wife Sabina. Born in Romania of Jewish decent. he became a believer in Jesus Christ as Messiah, daring to say that communism and Christianity were not compatible. For this he was imprisoned and tortured for over eight years. He was released only to be re-arrested a short time later and was imprisoned another seven years. He suffered unbelievable torture, beatings, starvation, solitary confinement with neither light nor window for three years. His wife Sabina was also arrested and forced to work in a slave labor camp for five years.

Richard was permanently released in the early 1960's after a church paid $10,000 ransom for him. In 1966 he testified before the US Senate's Internal Security Subcommittee about his imprisonment and torture in the then communist country of Romania. In front of TV cameras he took off his shirt and showed his many scars from torture. His book, *Tortured for Christ*, became an international best seller.

I had heard of this remarkable man through news media, Christian TV and had also read *Tortured for Christ*. It was now 1986, and Mike Barbera was pastoring the Church of the Good Shepherd. He was the one who approached me about hosting the Wurmbrands. I was overwhelmed at the honor. "I was thinking of their staying in the little guest house," Mike suggested.

"Oh, Mike, that's not nice enough, or large enough," I protested.

"You don't understand, Ouida," he said, "These people do not like to be put up in fancy places, elegant hotels or such. They do not like for people to squander money on them." He assured me that they were some of the most humble people I would ever meet.

The guest house was certainly a humble abode-- just the basics: a good king-size bed, night stand and lamp, shelves for books, a simple love-seat, tiny bath and small kitchen. It faced the round pedestal fountain. There was a concrete slab near the cottage that had once been the floor of the wash house. I used it to pot plants. I made it into a welcoming outdoor seating area with some chairs and additional plants and ferns.

The Wurmbrands stole my heart at first sight. Sabina was short, like me. They were probably in their seventies at this time. While I was in total awe of these giants of the faith, they made me feel at ease in my own home. I knew nothing about Sabina and had not read her book, "The Pastor's Wife" (which I now have an autographed copy). The thing that struck me about her right away was the way she showed respect to her husband. She was attentive to his every need, and at mealtime she served his plate, always making sure that the food was suitable to his diet. At times she called him Lord, like Sarah did Abraham in the Bible. They arrived on a Friday and stayed until Tuesday, so we did not get to have them speak on Thursday night, however all of our friends went to the churches where they were to speak and they were blessed.

Our grandson Jason who was then living with his father in New Orleans, was spending that weekend with us. I was glad he was there. At age 14 he was impressionable and what better example could he have than Richard Wurmbrand. On Saturday the local newspaper called and wanted to send a reporter out to interview the Wurmbrands. I shall never forget one thing that Richard said to the young aspiring reporter. "If you want to be a good journalist, you must read everything you can about everything."

The reporter's article in the paper was excellent and it was obvious he had been greatly impressed with this mighty man of God.

Pastor Wurmbrand's feet were in bad condition from having been repeatedly beaten on the bottoms while in prison. It had been many years before but his feet still bothered him so much that he could hardly stand to wear shoes. He spoke in several churches that weekend, and on Monday he spoke in a high school in Gulfport. He had their attention immediately when he said, "You have a bare-footed jailbird for your speaker today." You could have heard a pin drop in that place the entire time he spoke. He told of how he was put in a freezer and kept there until he was almost dead, then checked by a doctor and put back in the freezer again and again. He talked about what it was like to live in solitary confinement for three years in an underground cubicle, with no light or window. During those times he was so close to Jesus that he felt His very presence. Many young people made professions of faith after hearing him speak.

Jason and I were helping Sabina with the book table, where she was most generous, giving away many more books than she was selling. Jason had asked if he could skip school in New Orleans the first couple of days of that week to be with Pastor Wurmbrand. I was only too happy to allow him to do that. I felt they were life changing days for him. Pastor Wurmbrand wrote more than 18 books in English and other languages. It is my understanding that he spoke more than twenty languages.

What had the Tanners ever done to deserve the privilege of hosting these incredible servants of God? Nothing! We had dedicated our house to the Lord and it was His to use as He saw fit. He only asks for our availability. Did I sometimes get tired and weary of the stream of people who came and went at Merrywood? Yes, I'm only human and had more than my share of daily responsibilities, but I took to heart the scripture that says," Let us not lose heart in doing good, for in due season we shall reap if we do not grow weary- So then, while we have opportunity, let us do good to all men, and especially to those who are of the household of faith." (Galatians 9-10)

Chapter 29

"He Comforts in Tribulation"

In 1977, our daughter Debby gave birth to our first beautiful grand-daughter, Sarah Elizabeth, in Greenville, MS. Fortunately I was able to be with the little family when she was born. Kenny took care of his dad so I could go. It was the first time I had been away from Jim more than a single night, but we all survived.

Kenny had graduated from Mississippi State University with a BS degree in Business Administration and Food Technology. His first job was that of a quality control manager with a shrimp processing plant in Pascagoula, Mississippi, a fifty mile commute each way. He had to wear white clothes and boots, which were never white for more than a day. The briny smell of those clothes was nauseating and I hated his job almost as much as he did.

One evening Kenny brought home a girl for us to meet. She was very pretty with a perfect figure and a bubbly personality. Her name was Tammy D'Angelo and she was from Biloxi. Something about her made me think she might turn out to be Kenny's wife. And sure enough they announced their engagement soon afterward. I liked Tammy very much but her father was a prosperous club owner with a lot of diversified businesses in the Biloxi area. I was worried that Kenny might be getting into a lifestyle that was not in his best interest.

Nevertheless, we approved of the marriage. They were married in 1981. The reception was quite elaborate, complete with a champagne fountain. We had many out of town guests and local Christian friends in attendance, including a number of local pastors. At the reception, Mr. D'Angelo said to Jim, "Who knows? You might have me going to Sunday School before long." How we wished that could have happened.

Kenny went to work for his father-in-law who set up a delicatessen business for Tammy. In 1982 Kenny and Tammy were expecting their first child and had asked me to help them decorate the nursery. Three months before Tammy was due, Debby gave birth to our second granddaughter, Rachel, every bit as beautiful as her sister! I was relishing my role as grand-mother.

When Tammy went into labor, Kenny called to see if we could come be with them at the hospital in Biloxi. Tammy was having problems. After hours of labor, it appeared she could not deliver the baby normally and would need a C-section. Tammy's mother was beside herself with anxiety; so were the many girls from the night club who had gathered there for the birth. I thought that they seemed unusually upset over a birth by C-section. I tried to comfort Mrs. D'Angelo but to no avail.

Kenneth Moreland Tanner, Jr. was born healthy and robust, with a head of black hair. As I watched my son stroking the back of his new-born son I knew that this was a bonding moment that would never be forgotten. We did not realize that at the same time the birth was taking place an event instigated by the devil himself was also occurring.

Mr. D'Angelo had not shown up for the birth of his grandchild. I thought that was strange and soon learned why everyone was so anxious. Evidence indicated that Mr. D'Angelo had been abducted from his home and foul play was feared. The police had been called in immediately, but were not giving out any information. They were keeping this dreadful news from Tammy because she was utterly exhausted after the labor and surgery.

Thirty-six hours went by with no news of Tammy's father. Terror filled the D;Angelo home where several family members all slept in one bed, fearing the worst. Tammy was getting suspicious as to why her dad had not come to see her. She was told he had to go out of town on business. Kenny had to take over the business of the club so Mrs. D'Angelo could deal with the crisis at hand. Jim had his job so I spent a lot of time with Tammy at the hospital . Kenny stayed with her at night. We made sure the TV was never on the local news because reports were now surfacing about her father. Kenny was a nervous wreck.

The phone call finally came. "They've found him," Kenny said softly. "Can you come be with me when .I have to tell Tammy?" He did not want her to find out from the TV or newspaper which made it a big headline that Mr. D'Angelo was found dead in the trunk of his yellow Cadillac in a grocery store parking lot. The details were gruesome.

It was 3:30 AM when we arrived at the hospital. Tammy was sleeping and Kenny did not want to awaken her. We sat in the waiting room with our son, wishing that he did not have to bear such news to his wife. We prayed for him to have the strength he needed to deal with the situation. About 6:00 he went in and she was awake. He broke the news and then asked us to come in. In all my life, I have never seen such a look on a person's face--utter despair and sorrow unspeakable. Nausea overtook her--sadness so deep that it was hard to watch. A nurse gave her a sedative.

"Though I walk through the valley of the shadow of death, I will fear no evil, for thou art with me..."Psalm 23:4. Those words comforted me, but would they comfort Tammy?

There were arrangements to be made. Once again, I was alone with Tammy. Kenny was overburdened and got no sleep. She wanted to know the details about her dad but was in no condition to deal with it. Her doctor did not want her to go the funeral service, but she was adamant, so he allowed her to go in a wheelchair for a private viewing. We went with her. It was hard but at least she got to say goodbye.

When she was discharged, they went to their little house where they had the nursery ready for the baby. But there was no peace there. In fact, there was fear and terror. They received strange phone calls, even threats on Kenny's life, I found out later. We invited Kenny and Tammy to come and stay for a while. They took us up on the offer. Tammy leaned back in

Jim's recliner and said, "There's such peace in this house." Yes, there was peace and love and we showered them with it. How wonderful to get to take care of my beautiful new grandson also. He was a source of joy in the midst of a tragic situation. Kenny was gone a lot, helping run the clubs and other businesses. I had lots of quality time with Tammy. I read the Bible to her and prayed with her.

One night Tammy and I were alone in the living room and she began talking about her past. "I wish there was some way that I could forget about the past and start all over again," she said.

"You can," I told her. "The Bible tells us that 'so far as the east is from the west, so far does God remove our sins from us." (Psalm 103:12)

"Oh, I want that for myself," she cried. The Lord provided this wonderful opportunity for me to pray with her the sinner's prayer and she received her salvation with tears of joy. She walked over to the bassinet where her new son lay sleeping and said, "You've got a brand new mom." And she was! Immediately she began asking me about the Holy Spirit. She had been reading about the Holy Spirit in some literature upstairs and wanted to know more. The hour was late and we were both so tired. I gave her a book by Tom McKenney on the Holy Spirit and told her to read it for better understanding and we would discuss it later.

After Tammy went upstairs I woke up Jim, "Tammy got saved! Tammy got saved!" We rejoiced and he was off to sleep again, but I was not. I was too excited and couldn't wait for daylight so I could share the good news with others.

The circumstances around the death of her father were difficult for Tammy to deal with. She loved him so much. One day she came to me and said, "I wish my daddy could have been saved before he died." I shared a scripture with Tammy that I felt God had given me when we first received the awful news about him.

I Corinthians 5:5 (NAS) "I have decided to deliver such a one to Satan for the destruction of his flesh, so that his spirit may be saved on the day of the Lord Jesus".

Mr. D'Angelo had been born and raised in a Catholic home and saw to it that his family went to church on Holy Days. Since he had been tortured before being killed and with those deep Catholic roots, surely he had cried out to God during his horrible demise. This thought has given much comfort to Tammy over the years She has long since forgiven her father's killer and the parties involved and has since become a woman of deep faith.

A few months later Kenny and Tammy rented a house a couple of blocks away from us. He was searching for another job but was not interested in the field he had been trained in at Mississippi State. Kenny had always been good with his hands when it came to electronics. I suggested that perhaps he might want to take some training in that field. He ended up taking a two-year course in electronics and found himself in a good paying job with a major company. It meant relocating to Pensacola, Florida which is where they remain today.

As for Tammy's family: her mother moved to northeast Alabama to be near her own relatives. Tammy's sister, Gina, relocated there also and was a wonderful caregiver to her mother, who became gravely ill with diabetes. Mrs. D'Angelo gave her heart to Jesus, as did Gina. She lived long enough to see Tammy and Kenny's two other children born, Kevin, in 1985 and Kristy, in 1989.

I am richly blessed to have six beautiful grandchildren and a loving, supportive, and helpful daughter-in-law.

CHAPTER 30

"BIRTH AND DEATH"

In 1983 we found ourselves in search of a new church home. Following a disagreement concerning administrative procedure, we felt we could no longer remain part of our present church. It was heart-wrenching because of the great love we had for all involved. We visited different churches with good things to offer but were not lead to join any of them. A number of other folks who left the church when we did felt the same. A group of friends wanted to meet together, pray and seek God's direction on what to do next. As you might expect the meeting took place at Merrywood. The decision was made to continue meeting at Merrywood as we sought the Lord's guidance.

Now our home was having more meetings than ever. In addition to Thursday night prayer meetings, we now had Sunday morning and evening services, including School. Nearly every room in the house was put into service. Forty-five people attended the first service. Suddenly, we were a church whether we wanted to be one or not. We began looking for another place to meet.

A piece of property went up for sale just days after our search began. The unfinished house was located between Long Beach and Pass Christian, approximately three miles inland from the beach. The house was originally intended for a family with eight children, but ill health had prevented its completion. In its present state, the house could be easily remodeled to meet our needs..

Such was the beginning of the Church of the Good Shepherd. Elders were elected and a pastor we all knew and loved, Rev. Ray Powers was called as minister. The entire church body helped with the renovations, but the task took longer than anticipated. The strain was particularly hard on Jim and me.

My mother had a stroke during this time and was partially paralyzed. It was necessary for me to make frequent trips to help out with her in my home town of Waynesboro, 135 miles away. Mother had begged my father never to put her in a nursing home. A man always true to his word, he had promised. The responsibility of helping with her care fell to my siblings and me. Though we hired full-time care-givers, they had to have some time off and the family tended to her care in their absence. My brother and his wife who lived next door bore the brunt of the responsibility, but my sister Gwen and I wanted to pull our share of the load. I had to take Jim with me because I also had to care for him as well. We would go up on Friday and come back on Saturday evening, in time to set up the living room for Sunday services. It was one of the most stressful times of my life.

The church met in our home for nine months. We often laughed and said we birthed the church in our living "womb" (room). The fellowship of working together on the new church fostered a special bond among the members. Jim wanted to be a part of the ongoing work. I have pictures of him, paint brush in hand, staining the trim The building began to take shape. I led the women in a stained glass project creating small Christian symbols to be mounted at the tops of the windows in the sanctuary. The building looked like a church! Finally the work was completed and we gave an exhausted sigh of relief.

During this time, watching my mother dwindle away before my eyes had been emotionally draining. She had been our rock through the years, so cheerful and loving, a wonderful wife, mother and grandmother. Now she lay curled in a fetal position with a feeding tube down her throat. unresponsive to our efforts to reach her mind. It was heart-breaking and was especially hard on my dad. The last day that I visited with her I could tell she was worse and I put my face next to hers and said, "You are so sick, aren't you, Mama?"

She could not speak but a tear rolled out of her eye and down her cheek. This after nine months of no response. My heart ached to think of how imprisoned she had been in her body and mind all this time. That night when I got home my spirit anguished. I sat at the kitchen table and cried out, "How long, oh Lord, how long?" I let out a long agonizing cry. The clock on the microwave showed 11:20 PM. Within minutes the phone rang with the news from my brother that Mama was gone. She had left this earthly life at 11:20 PM

I had felt it. My spirit had been with my mother as she left that shell of a body and entered into her heavenly abode. My father's grief was deep. We visited him often and had him come to spend some time with us. He especially liked to watch the boats going in and out of the picturesque Pass Christian harbor.

Daddy died of a stroke two years later. He had been in intensive care for two weeks and the family was only allowed to see him a few minutes at a time. The day before he died a tornado struck the outskirts of Laurel and the wounded came pouring into the hospital. Daddy was moved into a private room because the emergency cases needed the intensive care unit. Our family was glad to have the opportunity to spend his last few hours gathered round him in that room. A peace came over his face as we embraced him in love and he took his leave of us.

CHAPTER 31

"STAINED GLASS WINDOWS"

Church of the Good Shepherd had two interim pastors, Ray Powers and Tom McKenney, who agreed to serve until God provided a full time minister. The church grew and prospered under them.

As we sought the Lord's will in finding a full time pastor, there was a person who came to everyone's mind, Mike Barbera. We knew him to be a man of great integrity and faith as well as one whose goal and vision were to serve where he felt the Lord's leading. At the time Mike was the pastor at a church in Tennessee. When we approached him with the offer, he was led by the Lord to come to Good Shepherd. Soon afterwards, Mike and Sally Cassagne, whom Mike had worked with in the TCC ministry in New Orleans, joined the Barberas in their ministry. Under the leadership of these godly men, the church flourished, and I am happy to say that the rift between the last church we were in was reconciled and healed. Once again proving the scripture in Romans 8:28 "And we know that in all things God works for the good of those who love Him , who have been called according to His purpose."

The church was outgrowing its small facilities and God opened doors for us to buy adjacent land and erect a larger building. During its construction, I felt God was telling me that we needed to think about stained glass windows for the church. I knew that we could not afford to have them commissioned by a professional glass artisan, but maybe we could make them ourselves. After all, we women had done a pretty good job on the small ones in the old building.

I began researching stained glass. I read books on making stained glass windows. I also visited a local stained glass artisan who offered a plethora of advice. She volunteered to order the materials we would need and let us have them at only 10% over her cost. I was revved up. Designs flowed through my mind and I began making colored sketches. I continued my research. I found an idea here and another there, and continued seeking advice from the stained glass artist. She kept me from making some major mistakes.

The plan was to have eight 2x8 foot windows in the sanctuary and one 4x6 foot window over the baptistery. Each would have a Christian symbol in its center surrounded by beautiful purple, royal blue and clear etched glass. I made colored sketches of all of the windows, figured up what the costs of the materials would be, and presented them to the church for approval. I also challenged the members to help create them, especially the men. The congregation overwhelmingly agreed to help and the entire project was sponsored financially that day.

In my research I had learned that it is of the utmost importance to have exact templates for cutting each piece of glass. The patterns had to fit together perfectly while leaving room for the caming or lead that would be used to separate the pieces and hold them together. This meant hours of measuring every piece that would go into each window and laying them on an overall pattern of the precise size. I worked on my dining room table night and day for weeks.

Finally it was time to begin the project. A friend offered the use of a masonry block building in her yard as a workshop. It was not very large, but we were grateful for its use. As I had hoped, the men came through. They excelled at cutting the glass, stretching the lead, and soldering the joints. The ladies worked tirelessly as well. When they weren't helping with the windows they were providing food. It was an exciting project and we worked day and night, because most of the time the men could only work at night. It was tiring but the Lord gave me supernatural strength to keep going. I still had my responsibilities at home and the specialized care of Jim.

We began the work in October, took time out for the Thanksgiving and Christmas holidays and were trying to get the windows finished before the dedication of the new church building set for January 20. As I look back, nothing short of a miracle helped us accomplish such a monumental undertaking. The day before the dedication, we still had four windows to finish, a seemingly impossible task. Sent by the providence of God for the completion of His work, my brother and his son arrived on the scene that day. In town to visit his daughter, they came by to look at our project. Both gifted in working with their hands, they jumped right in and were an invaluable asset. Had it not been for them, I don't know if we could have finished that night.

It was a cold and stormy night, as the Peanuts comic strip would say, that final night of working on the windows. Freezing cold, rare sleet pelted our little workshop and the winds howled. It was cold inside the building as well. Poor Jim would not leave me to go home and rest. He was so tired but he tried to do what he could to help....cleaning the glass, rallying our spirits, etc. As it got later and later, workers began to drop out and go home. I think they figured that there was no way we could finish- But we were so close! How could I stop now? All the weeks and months of exhausting work and to be so near the end. I couldn't let it go, I just couldn't. Even though we were almost completely out of some materials, I just couldn't quit. Please Lord Jesus, strengthen my tired body, stretch the materials. I was at the bottom of the bucket of glazing compound, or putty that went between the glass and the lead and kept it from falling apart. Without it I couldn't finish. Crawling around on the cold floor at 2:00 AM, 3:00AM, 4:00 AM, I looked for little round bits of the putty that might have fallen. God provided little pea-sized bits. Finally, the last polishing with Windex and they were done. Exhausted, Jim and I left for home at 5:30 and I got him into bed. At 6:30 after showering I fell into bed, only to get up again at 8:00.

The windows were hung at 8:30 and the dedication service was at 10:30! Somehow, I didn't feel the tiredness. I was exhilarated that the project was finished and by how beautiful the windows looked. The guest speaker for the dedication prayed over each window and the symbol it represented. The church had an open house that afternoon and my strength continued to hold out, thank you Jesus. Jim's also, bless his heart. Did we ever sleep hard that night!

In relating this story about the stained glass windows, I want to make sure that the glory goes to the Lord God Almighty! It was His inspiration that sparked the idea, that gave us the knowledge, that provided the place, the material, the man and woman power, the food, the energy, and the sheer strength to see it through. I was just an ordinary housewife, with virtually no knowledge of how to spearhead such a project but He was my source! If God is in the equation He will see it through. Those windows still have a story to tell as you will find out later.

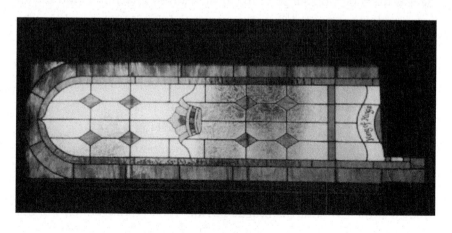

CHAPTER 32

"THE GIFT OF ART"

After moving to the coast, I was blessed to study under some outstanding artists and instructors. Alan Flattman of Covington, LA. is an outstanding pastel artist and recipient of the coveted Master Pastelists Award. Alan is represented by major galleries in the south. He has authored art books on pastels and been featured in various art magazines. Alan and his wife, Becky were our house-guests from time to time when he was teaching workshops in the area. I am so grateful to God for the opportunity He provided for me to take a workshop in Tuscany, Italy with Alan in my latter years.

Judi Betts of Baton Rouge, LA. is an incredible watercolor artist I was privileged to study under and host in my home. She too is widely known and leads workshops all over the world. I call her "happy eyes" because she is always smiling and makes her workshops such fun.

When I first saw Frank Janca doing a demonstration oil painting at an art gathering on the coast I was impressed. He painted in the style of the old masters with dark backgrounds and rich, luscious colors. He had studied at the Art Students League in New York. Though often working and traveling abroad, Frank was originally from Ocean Springs, MS. and

148

continued to visit the area when he could. I knew that Frank could help me become a better painter. We also became friends and he continues to visit at my home when he is in the country.

Once when I was wanting to study portraiture, I went to a local library to see what I could find. I was drawn to one book in particular, *Successful Portrait Painting* by John Howard Sanden. I had never heard of the artist before but I really liked his style, his method, and especially his terminology. I told my husband that I felt Mr. Sanden might be a Christian because of some of his remarks in the book. I was thrilled to have the book in my hands and began devouring its pages.

A couple of days later an artist friend of mine, Josephine Alfonso, called me and said, "Ouida, there is a National Portrait Seminar coming up soon in Washington, D.C. I want to go and I don't want to go by myself. I was wondering if you would like to go with me?" Would I ever, but I knew it would be almost impossible because of my role as Jim's caretaker. I told her so. "It's John Howard Sanden, " she said.

"What did you say? I can't believe it! I just checked his book out of the library and am studying it now," I replied in astonishment.

Josephine was sure Jim would want me to go and it would be a wonderful trip. We would fly and stay at a hotel on Capitol Hill, visit the art museums to our hearts' delight. It sounded too good to be true and I was sure it would be. In all the years since Jim's accident had put him in the wheelchair, I had never had a vacation away from him. I knew how hard it would be on him to have someone else take care of him, and who would? I felt guilty even thinking about it, but I could not contain my excitement when I told him about the seminar.

To my disbelief he said, "Maybe we can arrange it." He planned for his parents to come care for him in my absence and I found myself on a plane bound for the nation's capital.

When we arrived at our hotel in Washington, there was a lovely floral arrangement in my room from Jim, another wonderful surprise. The seminar was well organized and executed. There were talks and demonstration portraits by many different artists. That night I sat in a formal evening gown at a lovely banquet table with classical music playing while I conversed with some of the nicest people I had ever met. I kept thanking the Lord over and over for this glorious gift. I felt so loved by the Lord. Only He could have planned something so wonderful, so fulfilling.

I wrote a note to the Sandens thanking them for the gracious manner in which the seminar was conducted and included a scripture that I felt was appropriate. "A man's gift makes room for him and brings him before great men." Proverbs 18:16 (KJV). Indeed John Sanden was a gifted man who had done portraits of important people all over the world.

Little did I know the best was yet to come. A convocation ceremony was held on Sunday morning before the seminar concluded. John Howard said, "Now I am going to give you the three most important ingredients in a portrait: #1 Creative Meditation- take time to be alone, listen to good music, read scripture, read poetry, get your mind in a creative state. #2 Creative Prayer: Ask God to guide you, to give you divine inspiration as you paint, etc. #3 Creative Worship – Praise the Lord for His gift of creation, of salvation, His wonderful love for His children. Mr. Sanden elaborated much more on all of these "ingredients".

My heart was soaring! I felt wrapped in God's love. What a wonderful gift He had given me in this seminar. I have never felt His presence stronger than that time. Since then I have attended two more of Mr. Sanden's seminars, and they have been equally great. But that first one was my Heavenly Father's special gift to me.

I never had an art studio or a good place in which to paint. I had very little time to myself as it was. When I did find time to paint, I had to clear out a place in a corner of a room to set up my easel and supplies. But over the years I had kept at it, squeezing in a few hours here and there. I was involved in several art organizations on the coast, even serving as president of the Gulf Coast Art Association and the Pass Christian Art Association. I attended workshops when I could and even taught a few myself. I had been approached about teaching art lessons on a regular basis, but because I didn't have facilities in which to work, I had to decline.

When I returned home from the seminar, more than ever I wanted a place to paint and God blessed me once again. The original owner of Merrywood had built a library behind the main house and its big backyard. It was quite large, having a long room, with ten windows and a fireplace. There was a small office, a bedroom, small bath and kitchen, and an idyllic screened in side porch overlooking what at one time had been a long reflecting pool swimming with koi. A show place in its day, it now sat neglected needing paint and repairs. Mr. Bell's daughter, Alice Prindeville, who was in her late eighties had lived in the library since her father's death. A widow, Alice was experiencing financial difficulties. Her lawyer approached us about the possibility of buying the house from Alice with her having life-estate privileges until her death. It was her desire to see the property rejoined because she was pleased with the way we had resurrected Merrywood. It would be ten years before we gained possession of the library but oh, what an asset it was.

The place was in rough condition when it came into our possession. The first Thanksgiving after we got it, I met my family with paint brushes and buckets of soft greenish gray paint. What a weekend we had, and what a help to me. Much more was still needed- new heating and air, outside repairs, new plumbing, etc. but finally it was done. My very own studio! At long last. The joy it brought me was unbelievable. Jim enjoyed long hours there also as he was now retired from his job at the hospital.

I had the place prayed over, anointed with oil and dedicated to the Lord, and truly His Spirit resided there. I began teaching art classes and the place was so inspirational that often my students did not want to leave. My own painting improved in my new retreat and I created some of my best paintings there. The studio also became another guest house, much bigger and nicer than the little cottage. Some of the artists I mentioned earlier were often guests there and loved it because they could also paint during their stay on the lovely gulf coast.

The most ambitious painting I had ever undertaken was painted in my new studio. A large rendering of the "Throne Room in Heaven" taken from Revelation 5:4 -5. I did a lot of researching but could find almost nothing on the subject. In my collection of art books and religious books there were a lot of religious paintings but almost none on the throne room. I prayed diligently for inspiration, played Christian music and anything I thought would lift my thoughts to heavenly realms. "The HALLELUJAH

CHORUS" came closer than anything else. I worked on the painting for two years off and on. It was painted in oils which allowed me to do so. When it was finally done, the painting was well received. I had prints made which were often used in Revelation Bible studies.

Those years having my own studio were some of the most rewarding of my life. It wasn't just any studio- it was the setting, the history of the man who wrote so much of his life's work there, the beautiful foliage of bamboo, live oak trees and blooming plants that made it so inviting. It was a place of tranquility. The light streaming through its many windows, the crackling fire in the winter months, the smell of spice tea or coffee, all contributed to my contentment there. Truly the presence of the Lord was in that place, and how I thanked Him.

CHAPTER 33
"FOR BETTER OR FOR WORSE:
FIFTY YEARS TOGETHER"

The time finally came when we felt it best to close down the Thursday night prayer meetings. There were many church activities going on, and we were getting a little weary after some twenty-three years of regular meetings in our home. We remained busy with the Lord's work and with our hospitality role. During this time, we became attached to a wonderful elderly couple who often spoke at Good Shepherd. Bill and Delores Winder were from Shreveport, Louisiana and had an active ministry in Bible teaching and healing services. Delores, herself, was miraculously healed at a Holy Spirit Conference in Dallas, Texas, where noted faith healer and evangelist Kathryn Kuhlman was ministering. Terminally ill and in a body cast for fourteen years, Delores received much more than a physical healing; she was set free from doubts about the supernatural things of God. Since then she and Bill had been on numerous television programs, led conferences in many churches and written a book about their experience, *Joy Cometh in the Morning.*

They became very dear friends and often visited us at Merrywood. Bill was a real handy man and never left without making necessary repairs around the house. Jim often said that if he had never believed in miracles before he met Delores Winder, he would have believed in them after hearing her testimony, realizing the seriousness of her physical condition and the improbability of her healing.

It may seem that our lives were one big happy time of hosting great Christians and basking in fellowship. In truth, we had more than our share of hardships, family problems, illnesses, deaths, and disappointments. Jim battled many health issues that commonly plague paraplegics.

I myself had a number of surgeries and suffered from periodontal disease and hypertension. My worst problem was that my back would slip out of joint from time to time, the result of lifting the heavy wheelchair and helping Jim with his daily needs. Overall though, God kept me going and provided me with a high metabolism and lots of energy.

As Jim's parents grew older, they were beset with major health issues. We had to make frequent trips to Mobile hospitals and eventually nursing homes. In time, Gretchen, Jim's mother, died from a stroke. His father, Kenneth, survived her but suffered from dementia and circulatory problems which caused him to lose both his legs before his death several years later.

One of the greatest trials for our family came in 1999, when our grandson Kevin was involved in a horrific automobile accident. At age fourteen, Kevin was being driven home from school by a friend. She failed to negotiate a curve, ran off the road, hit a culvert and turned her pickup truck upside down. She was unharmed but Kevin lay trapped underneath the vehicle. He suffered a traumatic brain injury and remained in a coma for several weeks. His recovery was slow, requiring extensive speech and physical therapy. Today Kevin is in college and working a full time job. How we praise God for His awesome power to heal and restore.

Another tribulation for us was a freak accident in which Jim broke both his legs below the knees. We were on the beach highway heading to our home when a long-bodied truck hauling building materials made a sudden stop while trying to make a sharp right turn. I was not driving very fast and was able to stop without hitting the truck. I didn't even hear Jim when he slid out of his electric wheelchair and his legs crumpled beneath him. We went immediately to the emergency room but it was hours before he got the attention he needed. Because Jim could not move his legs, his doctors felt it better not to put him in regular casts and used flexible Velcro ones. He had to spend that night in the hospital, but I was not allowed to stay with him.

At home I was in turmoil. Though I could not have prevented the accident, I felt guilt ridden because I was driving. I was upset with Jim because he had not used the seat belt to secure himself to his wheelchair. He would not have fallen out if he's been strapped in. I felt nauseated as I sat on our bed and tried to make sense of what was happening, praying all the while. I thought of the scripture in Lamentations 3:33, "God does not willingly bring affliction or grief to the sons of men."

What else did it say in Lamentations 3, I wondered? I opened my Bible to verse 1, "I am the man who has seen affliction….." Verse 4, "He has made my skin and flesh grow old, and HAS BROKEN MY BONES." God was there with us. My solace was knowing that He would see us through this just like He had brought us through so many trials before.

Following the accident, Jim's care became even more difficult. His legs could not be bent at all and had to remain completely straight. It took extra hands to help him in and out of his wheelchair. Special leg rests had to be installed on his chair. He couldn't turn in the bed to relieve pressure on his back, and he was perfectly miserable. We had to hire extra help and depend on good friends like Warren Jones and David Edmonds to help us out.

My heart goes out to all who have to cope with these kinds of situations. There are many who face similar problems on a daily basis. I think of handicapped people all over the world who have to rely on others for their most basic needs. I think of the hundreds of thousands of nurses and caregivers who attend these patients, and the weariness and frustrations they live with consistently. I think of all of our veterans coming back from war who are having to learn to live with debilitating sicknesses and injuries. I think of the wives who are facing a multitude of problems in adjusting to their new and difficult roles as care givers.

I was glad that Jim had chosen to specialize in Rehabilitation medicine. His patients loved him because truly he understood their plight. He was 'one of them'. They trusted him and would abide by his advice. To show their gratitude, they liked to provide him with fresh vegetables and one fellow in particular, Eddie Necaise, supplied us with enough to fill our freezer for the winter months. Jim would sometimes come home with a homemade cake or signature dish from the wife or mother of a patient, their way of saying thank you for his compassion and care to their loved one.

Weeks went by as we nursed his broken legs and spirit too. He was getting older and his condition had taken a toll on him. He developed more urinary tract infections, coming down with one severe bout that nearly killed him. Thank God that our daughter Dawn along with her college age son, Jason had come to live with us during those last few years They were a tremendous support and source of joy for both Jim and me.

Our 50th wedding anniversary was coming up soon and Jim's legs still could not be bent at the knees. We had planned on having a big celebration but now that seemed impossible. Dawn, however, was determined we would commemorate the day with a big party. She began making plans, enlisting help from a lot of our friends. She even talked the doctor into letting Jim's legs be bent for the couple of hours for the party. Our son Kenny, his wife Tammy and their children came from Pensacola and helped with the preparations

It was a beautiful day with warm breezes from the gulf. Our hydrangeas were in full bloom making a beautiful background for the white tables and chairs set in the grass. Lush ferns surrounded the round fountain which had been cleaned out and was splashing fresh water. Big oak trees offered plenty of shade for the guests. A dear friend, Janet Gillingham, made the gorgeous mandarin orange cake that was in several tiers and topped with fresh flowers. Other dear friends helped with the food and punch. Friends from church, the prayer group, relatives and neighbors came to celebrate with us.

Pastor Mike Barbera offered some fitting remarks and led us in the renewal of our wedding vows. Dawn read a lovely poem and Mike Ramsey sang for us. It was all so nice, so appropriate and the presence of the Lord could be felt by all. No banquet hall could have had the ambience of the place, our home for nearly thirty years. I will forever treasure the memories of that day.

Jim gave me a beautiful gold watch and earrings as an anniversary gift, with a little shopping help from Dawn. I gave him a gold watch. But the greatest gift of all was the love that we had shared for those fifty years. Ours had been an unusual marriage. There were some very difficult times and many joyous times. It seemed the years had passed all too quickly.

CHAPTER 34

"THE MORNING OF 911"

By September Jim finally had the Velcro casts removed. Life was returning to normal. After what we had been through with the broken legs, the daily routine didn't seem so hard anymore. We were able to get out for drives now and Jim was glad to be able to go to church again.

One morning our phone rang early and Dawn's voice said. "Do you have your TV on?" The date was 9/11/2001. How many times have you heard people ask if you knew where you were on 9/11. We were still in bed and quickly turned on the TV. A plane had just flown into one of the World Trade Center towers! Oh, no, now another plane had hit the second tower! What on earth was happening? Were we in a war? The Pentagon was hit by a third plane and then the news that another plane had crashed in Pennsylvania. We joined the world in watching the worst terrorist attack our nation had ever known.

How could this happen? The United States had supposedly the strongest military force in the world. How could anything this horrendous have breached our invisible boundaries? It was unthinkable! Like millions of others we were glued to the TV. The images were horrifying: the burning towers, people jumping out of windows, people screaming and running for their lives from the gigantic, billowing cloud of debris racing through the streets. Heart-wrenching stories of death and devastation along with heart-warming stories of brave first responders filled our minds during restless nights. Who did this? And why?

We've had some answers since then – not good, but enlightening in that we now know who our enemies are. I have heard so many people say, "Where was God when the towers went down? When the planes crashed?

No doubt He was there, though most did not perceive Him. There are many scriptures that could be applied to the tragedy. But the question remains "why?" I believe that God has removed His hedge of protection from America, because she has left her first love, her trust in God, in His laws, in His love. We had taken prayer out of schools and now schools have been the targets of mass shootings. We are paying a very high price for rebelling against God.

"Have you not brought this on yourselves by forsaking the Lord your God?" Jeremiah 2:17.

"Your wickedness will punish you; your backsliding will rebuke you. Consider then and realize how evil and bitter it is for you when you forsake the Lord your God and have no awe of me," declares the Lord, the Lord Almighty. Jeremiah 2:19.

"Who can speak and have it happen if the Lord has not decreed it? Is it not from the mouth of the Most High that both calamities and good things come? Why should any living man complain when punished for his sins? Let us examine our ways and test them, and let us return to the Lord." Lamentations 3:37-40. (NIV)

A heaviness hung over the nation for months in the aftermath of the 9/11 tragedy.

CHAPTER 35

"LAST DAYS"

Jim's health had been declining since the broken legs. His breathing became more labored and his doctor suggested the use of oxygen when needed. His blood pressure elevated which was unusual for him. He still pushed himself to keep going, especially to church.

We had planned to take a vacation to visit Debby and Lewis in South Carolina in June of 2003, but I just didn't see how Jim could possibly hold out to make the long trip. He very much wanted to go because he loved sitting on their back porch overlooking their small lake. I wanted to go for an additional reason. Pastor Benny Hinn, the widely known TV healing evangelist, was going to be holding a crusade in Greenville, South Carolina, only fifty miles from Debby's house. I still clung to the hope that Jim would be healed of his paralysis after more than forty-two years in the wheelchair. He had already out-lived his life expectancy by thirty-one years.

We made the decision that if Jim's health improved and his blood pressure returned to normal, we would attempt the trip. We would take the oxygen tank along just in case. We asked Dawn to make the trip with us and things went well. No problems traveling or while we were at Debby's house.

160

We also made the trip to Greeneville and the Benny Hinn Crusade. As expected the crowd was huge, and also as expected, there were hundreds of handicapped people. There was lots of praise and worship. Many of Benny Hinn's prayer team spread throughout the large coliseum even as he preached and prayed for people on stage.

My heart was pounding as one of the team leaders laid hands on Jim and began praying fervently. When he moved on to others Jim turned to me with tears in his eyes and said, "I'm sorry, Ouida." He had made the trip for me. He wanted to be healed for my sake, not his. He was tired and weary from the long struggle and was ready to go on and be with Jesus.

His health continued to hold the rest of the trip and all the way home. After a few days at home his blood-pressure spiked and he needed the oxygen again. It had been two weeks since the trip. God supernaturally upheld him during that time, whether it was for Jim or me, I don't know.

July 4, 2003, arrived --time for our annual Fourth of July backyard cookout. This year we were going to have most of the Tom McKenney family with us for the day. It had been a long time since we had been able to celebrate together with these dear friends. We had others too, Bill and Penny Frith, Warren Jones, and two of Dawn's friends from Memphis, Dr. Clifton Woolley and his daughter Marty. Kenny and his family were there. Debby and Lewis had stayed in South Carolina where Lewis' mother was extremely ill in the hospital. It was a rainy day and we had to set up the grill under the carport to cook the hamburgers and hot-dogs. We ate indoors and Jim Tanner ate a burger, hot-dog and home-made ice cream with much gusto. This meal, some of his favorite foods, would be his last.

CHAPTER 36

"TOMORROW, TOMORROW, I DIE"

Saturday morning, July 5, 2003: The first thing Jim said to me that morning as I was bending over the bed, adjusting his oxygen tube was, "Tomorrow...tomorrow..."

"What about tomorrow?" I asked.

"Tomorrow, I die."

I couldn't believe what I was hearing, but I also knew he wasn't joking. "No, honey, no!" I exclaimed, "I'm calling an ambulance!" I was aware of signs that he was degenerating before my eyes- practically no urinary output in the last twenty-four hours, the labored breathing, the dry lips.

I reached for the phone. "NO!" He was emphatic! "I am NOT going to the hospital. I don't want any more tubes or needles in me; No more heroic efforts. I just want to rest....," his voice trailed off. I couldn't stand by and watch this happen. I called Dawn at the little guest house, now her home. Distraught, she came quickly. She agreed, we needed to do something.

Our good friend, Dr. Bill Hopper was vacationing in North Carolina, but I called him. "It's O.K. for someone to die at home if that's what he wants," he said in response to my question of "what to do?" We still had family and company in town for the holiday weekend. We all agreed that we needed to DO SOMETHIING.

But, as we now say, Jim dug in those paralyzed heels and refused to go or have any medical help come. He slept a lot, the oxygen machine humming away. I called our precious daughter, Debby, in South Carolina. I also called Mike Barbera, Jim's brother Bill , Tom McKenney, and Jim's good friend Bill Frith, who rarely missed a day visiting. His long-time friend from the VA, Eddie Necaise, came and tried to act cheerful, but like all the others that were coming and going he, too, thought this might be it and didn't want to make light of the day. Jim recognized them and thanked them for coming, then drifted off to sleep between visits. When Pastor Sam Clark went in to pray for him, he came out shaking his head and said, "I went in to pray for him and he ended up praying for me and my family."

As for me, it was one of the hardest days of my life, another of those surreal times. I was ridden with guilt at not doing anything for Jim in terms of life-saving measures. I did what I could to make him comfortable, moistening his lips with water, adjusting his pillows. I didn't want to go against his will and put him in the hospital. I knew how much he loved Merrywood and could understand his wanting to stay home as long as possible.

And so the day slowly passed with little changes in Jim's condition. He slept a lot, laboriously, the oxygen humming away, no doubt sustaining his life. Family members drifted in and out of the room, anxious but not wanting to appear so in order to keep everyone's spirit up including Jim's. But a cloud seemed to hang over us all.

The guys went fishing off and on at the nearby pier but their hearts were not in it. We busied ourselves with chores, but underneath the surface, doubts and fears were there. As night settled in, Kenny and Tammy decided to take Kristy to the fishing rodeo in Gulfport, a family tradition during the 4th of July holidays. Dawn went down to her cottage to shower and rest. Jason went upstairs and said he was going to read a while and would be down later.

And so it was Jim and me, alone together in what would be the waning hours. He drifted in and out of sleep. I needed to get him out of his clothes, but he was too weak to help. "Call Jason," he said. I went halfway up the stairs and called, several times but couldn't arouse him from a deep sleep. I struggled with the clothes myself until finally they were off.

Dawn called and asked if her dad was asleep. When told yes, she said in that case she would go on to bed. Kenny and family had not yet come in from the fishing rodeo.

There was the usual routine of hooking up the urinary bedside bag, however there was still no urine output. I tried to get him to drink some water but he refused, even though his lips were dry and cracking. I sponged them off with a wet cloth. "My neck hurts," he said. I heated the neck pillow in the microwave and placed it under his head.

As I was adjusting his pillows, his hand reached out and touched one of my breasts. An accident I thought. Jim had long since caressed my body. But the hand then went to the other breast. A lump caught in my throat. Was he telling me something? Sending me a message? It was a love language, one of the most beautiful things he could possibly have done. Immediately my mind recalled the scripture in Proverbs 5:18-19, "Rejoice in the wife of your youth- a loving doe, a graceful deer. May her breasts satisfy you always. May you ever be captivated by her love."

Yes, he was sending me a message, a message of love. Because we were one in the spirit, God's spirit, he knew that I would get the meaning of what he was trying to say. He was telling me that even in the midst of death, my love comforted him, the touch of my breasts satisfied him. How beautiful! I kissed the dry lips over and over, kissed his forehead, re-warmed the pillow, repositioned his legs. As weariness settled over my own tired body, I laid close beside him, not sleeping- listening, rising every few minutes to do something for him.

Kenny, Tammy and Kristy came in quietly, said goodnight and went upstairs. I was up every few minutes checking on Jim. I thought I heard what is called the 'death rattle', but I didn't want to believe it. The oxygen machine drowned out a lot of sounds in the room.

About 4:30 in the morning as I wearily crawled back into my side of the bed, I heard him say something to me that I didn't understand. I only remember that his voice sounded stronger, more youthful, like when we first married. I thought to myself, *He sounds so much better, so strong...* I felt a surge of relief and peace sweep over me, and in my exhaustion I fell into a deep sleep.

Little did I know that those would be his last words to me. And oh, how I wish I could have understood them, could replay them. Was he telling me goodbye? Why can't I remember? Only in heaven will I know.

The Lord knew I needed to sleep. The alarm went off at 8:30. It was Sunday morning, time to get ready for church, time to reach for Jim's hand and our usual prayer time together. His head was almost on my pillow, the oxygen still going. I reached for the hand that was stretched out alongside me. It looked pale, but then it often did lately. It felt cool, but that wasn't too unusual either. I rubbed the hand- no response- the thought entered my mind, could he be gone? I didn't want to know. I wanted to forestall the probability. I held the hand, but I feared the truth. Slowly, my eyes moved upward to his face- the parted lips that had grown cold. I sat up-right, hoping against hope, but it was all too real. "He meant what he said, 'tomorrow I die', I said to myself. How did he know? Did Jesus tell him? Did he know because he was a doctor and the signs were there? One thing I know, HE knew.

I kissed the cold lips, the closed eyes. My tears pooled in his closed eyes, making it appear he was crying too. Was he? I had my own moment of heart-wrenching grief, then went to the phone to call Dawn. By the time I walked to the back door she was there in her pajamas, tears streaming down her face; up in the bed with her daddy, calling him, trying to get him to come back, then upstairs to awaken the others.

I dialed 911. "Do you need an emergency vehicle?" they asked. I told them I thought he was already gone. They came anyway.

I didn't realize that Kenny and Jason had gotten up early and had gone fishing. They had walked through our bedroom, heard the oxygen running and thought everything was O.K., that we were asleep.

Frantically they arrived, as did the paramedics. Mike Barbera came. For some reason he had already asked Pastor Sam to preach for him that morning. He wept by the side of the bed, "My brother, my friend," he kept saying. Even the funeral home attendants were moved, they who had seen so much.

Our little Korean friend, Penny Frith, an ordained minister, arrived and climbed into the bed hovering over the lifeless form. "Wake up, Dr. Jim, get up, please wake up!" she was shouting. I put my arm around her and pulled her away.

"It's no use, Penny, he's gone home."

I didn't want to see him leave our room, this house that he so loved, for the last time. It was almost unbearable. Is anyone ever ready to let go? The phone calls began. First our beloved daughter Debby, in South Carolina, having to receive the news without the comfort of the rest of the family. My heart ached for her. My children took over notifying relatives and close friends.

I managed to get dressed and composed myself somewhat, but with each loving face that came through the door with open arms, fresh grief washed over me. Reality settled in. Things had to be done, decisions made. Tom McKenney was quick on the scene, a forever friend, doing what friends do.

The body of Christ swung into action. My dear friend, Brenda Rolison , was such a blessing. She came over and took incoming phone calls, greeting those who arrived as food began to pour in. News of Jim's death had spread quickly. It was late evening before the family was alone. Dawn wanted to sleep with me that night. She needed comforting. We cuddled and cried and slept.

Hundreds of people attended the visitation the night before the funeral, standing in long lines to speak to the family. It was very touching, so many from so far. Jim's brother, Bill, was the first to come, his visit was brief, his words few. He was hurting. I could hardly believe that our dear friends, Pastor Gary Thibodeaux and his wife, Susan, had come all the way from Texas for the service. Gary had spent hours studying the Bible with Jim in our living room. I was also surprised to see our business agent from A.G. Edwards there. He had never met Jim, but after seeing the wonderful article in the local newspaper, he wanted to see for himself this man who was so highly esteemed.

It was hot, July 9, the day of the funeral, but thank God, no rain. The Church of the Good Shepherd was packed. What a range of emotions I was experiencing. I had such gratitude for the out-pouring of relatives and friends who had traveled so far, for the many who had attended our Thursday night prayer meetings over the years, Jim's patients; a real cross-section of people from near and far.

The services lasted two hours, yet passed quickly. Linda Gammel sat at the piano, playing many of Jim's favorites. The congregation joined together in singing "We Have Come Into This House", a song we used to open our Thursday night meeting with. "No sad songs at my funeral." Jim had often said, "I want uplifting music." He would have loved hearing the quartet of friends who sang a medley of his gospel favorites, "When the Roll is Called Up Yonder", "No Tears in Heaven", "When We All Get to Heaven," "Just a Little Talk With Jesus Makes it Right".

Our son, Kenny, gave a beautiful tribute to his father, sharing happy times and honoring Jim's strong Christian influence in his own life. There was hardly a dry eye in the house. Our "adopted son' Mike Ramsey sang, "People Need the Lord", also one of Jim's songs and what a message he carried.

A former pastor, Rev. Howard Beam, shared in the eulogy, along with Pastor Mike Barbera, obviously shaken because of his great affection for Jim. Our forever friend, Tom McKenney gave the closing remarks, wrapping it all up with an appropriate altar call.

At my request. Allen Young sang the very popular song at the time, "I Can Only Imagine". Some of the words being, "Will I dance before you Jesus, or will I be able to speak at all?"

A live oak tree spreads its long limbs over the grave-site in the Pass Christian Live Oak Cemetery, providing shade for that day and in the years to come.

CHAPTER 37

"A GRIEF SO REAL"

I did not expect my grief to be so intense. After all, I had lived with the possibility of an early death for Jim since his accident forty-two years before. But now his absence was all too real. I thought I heard him call my name time after time. I kept expecting him to come rolling around a corner of a room in his wheelchair. Nights were especially hard. The absence of his body in bed beside me. No hand to hold in the mornings when we normally prayed together. His empty place at the head of the table. I missed him in the kitchen where he often sat and talked to me while I cooked. I longed to hear his laughter, the sound of his voice.

And oh, how I missed him at church. He always sat in the center aisle, for obvious reasons. I fought back tears when I looked at his empty place beside me. His last Sunday there little Ella Grace, who always sat in the row right in front of us and loved to dance in the aisle to the worship music, had turned around and sat down on his feet, promptly untying his shoes. I'll never forget the look he gave me with a twinkle in his eye. That gesture will linger with me the rest of my life.

How was I going to cope with the memories that consumed me? I spent a lot of time in my art studio. It became more of a sanctuary than ever. I felt closer to God in that studio than anywhere else. Now I could talk out loud to Him, listen to music and cry. Many songs brought back memories and tears flowed. One such song was "Softly as I Leave You"

> Softly, I will leave you softly,
> For my heart would break
> If you should wake and see me go.
>
> So I leave you softly,
> Long before you miss me;
> Long before your arms can beg me stay
> For one more hour, for one more day.
>
> After all the years,
> I can't bear the tears to fall.
> So softly I will leave you there, I will leave you there.

Indeed, Jim had left me softly. He had not writhed or cried out in pain. He had simply faded away softly, drifting in and out of sleep, not asking for help of any kind. When I awoke in the morning to find his head on my pillow, I felt he was letting me know he was saying goodbye… leaving me softly.

What was the matter with me? I was a woman of deep faith, made even deeper because of the common bond of faith Jim and I had shared. I knew he was better off, no longer paralyzed, had no suffering of any kind. I could imagine him rejoicing in the presence of his beloved Jesus; the re-union with dear loved ones who had gone on before him. I would never want to call him back from such glory! Why, then, could I not get a grip on my emotions?

It was the absence- the awful absence-the loneliness without him. Dawn and Jason were still living at Merrywood and the guest house. They too, felt his absence. We tried to comfort each other. Debby spent some time with us, too, but couldn't stay long because her mother-in-law was still very ill back in South Carolina. My sister Gwen came and spent special time with me. What a comfort she was.

I found myself missing some of the routine "duties" that I used to dread-- like emptying Jim's urinal bag and putting the sheep-skin heel cushions on his feet at bedtime. Now I wished I could do all those things again, just to have him back. Half of me was missing. When the Bible says, concerning marriage, "Two shall become one.", and one of them is missing, how could you not feel the loss?

Our family received many beautiful floral arrangements and potted plants in memory of Jim. They were all lovely and deeply appreciated but one completely overwhelmed me, both in its beauty and its size. Sent by a family friend in Boston, it stood nearly four feet tall. A huge spiral shaped vase held white hydrangeas, white roses, white star-gazer lilies, blue delphiniums, and other beautiful filler flowers. It cried out to be painted.

And paint it, I did. In the quietness of my studio, I painted and listened to music-all kinds of music- classical, spiritual songs, love songs- I painted and I listened and I cried. I began to heal. The Holy Spirit, the "Comforter" came and did what Jesus said He would do in John 14:26.

My 71st birthday was coming up less than a month after Jim died. My friends wanted to give me a nice party, but I didn't feel like celebrating. At their suggestion, I agreed to a simple luncheon at Brenda Rolison's house. It was lovely. My friends were loving and comforting. I noticed a beautiful arrangement of red roses in the middle of the round dining table. When we had finished eating, Sally Cassagne placed the red roses before me along with a card, and said, "These are from Jim."

A lump caught in my throat and my eyes filled with tears. Sally encouraged me to open the card and read it aloud. "Dear Ouida"... The card was so personal I could hardly believe it. The words went on to say how much he had appreciated all that I had done for him over the years; how he knew he had not expressed his thankfulness enough; how much he loved me and wished he could be there for the party. The words sounded so much like him, I choked as I read them and had to stop and wipe away the tears many times. There were no dry eyes around the table.

"The Lord told me to do this, Ouida. I can assure you this thing is from God. He put the thought in my mind, and spoke the words from Jim into my heart.," Sally assured me. I knew that, of course. It was like a footnote to a beautiful love-story. What my friends did not know was that red roses were Jim's favorite flowers and when he sent me flowers for special occasions, they were almost always red roses. Also, and something that no-one there could have known was that in our dating years, Jim would always play the very popular song on the juke-box, "Red Roses for a Blue Lady." Our God is such a personal God. He knows our every need.

CHAPTER 38

"LIFE GOES ON"

There was much to do in the weeks and months that followed. The grief didn't go away, but it began to soften somewhat. I had heard often that "time" is a great healer. And it is true. When emotions are raw, it is difficult to lay aside our grief- but with the love and support of family and friends, we realize that life must go on. We have no recourse. Not only for ourselves, but for other family members, friends and acquaintances.

One of the first steps to "letting go" of my grief was to sell the handicapped van. I bought a new Ford Taurus station wagon which would be perfect for hauling my art equipment around and for traveling, which I hoped to do in the future.

Dawn and I felt the need to get away from the sadness and sorrow that lingered at Merrywood. We decided to take a road trip to visit Debby and Lewis in South Carolina where their lake would reflect the beautiful fall foliage. From there we traveled east into Virginia. I had always loved that beautiful state, and it was refreshing to once again enjoy the sights.

We visited my dear friends, Dr .Charles Homan and his wife Rose, in Virginia Beach. Also known for their gift of hospitality they hosted us to a delightful candlelight dinner as we remembered old times.

A day in Williamsburg was delightful, bringing back happy memories of visits there when we lived in Richmond. Our next stop was in Richmond and visits with dear friends Fred and Marion McCall and Dr. Billy Stuart and his wife Janet. Dr. Stuart had been Jim's personal physician when we lived there and we had kept in touch through the years. Again, I thank God for Christmas cards that keep people in touch with one another.

The trip was good for Dawn and me, although we both shed a few tears along the way as we recalled memories of by-gone days when we were together as a family. It was hard just thinking of our first Christmas without Jim. It had always been such a happy celebration for us, lots of beautiful decorations, parties, friends coming and going. Debby suggested that our entire family spend Christmas together at their house in South Carolina. Some of their friends had planned something very special for Christmas Eve--a hayride through thick woods to a small rustic cabin where hot soup and apple cider awaited us. It was a bitter cold night with thousands of stars glittering in the navy blue sky. A bonfire helped us to keep warm in what was truly a setting out of a Currier and Ives painting. A night to remember.

And so, the first Christmas without Jim came and went, and we survived.

Dr. Jim Tanner, on his graduatuon from University of Tennessee Medical School, 1954

Ouida Trigg
Miss Waynesboro High School
Waynesboro, MS
1951

Jim and Ouida, courting days
1950-51

Captain James Tanner in
paratrooper gear,
101st Airborne Division
Fort Campbell, KY
1956

Capt. James Tanner
Medical Officer
506 Infantry Division
101st Airborne
Fort Campbell, KY
1956-58

Above: Dr. Tanner receiving award from from vets at Veterans Administration Hospital, Biloxi, MS. Below left: Dr. Tanner with patient, Vernon Magee; VA hospital, Biloxi, MS

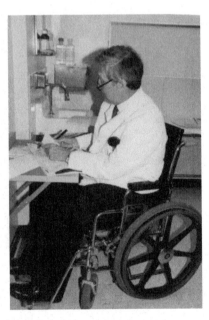

Above: Tanner family home, 1972-2007

Below, the Tanner family, left to right: Kenny, Dawn, Dr. Jim, Ouida, and Debby.

Above: Ouida with art students at Merrywood Art Studio, Pass Christian, MS.

Right: The artist takes a tea break.

Below: The artist at work.

original oil painting   "THRONE ROOM IN HEAVEN"   Ouida Tanner
72"48"   Revelation 4 and 5

The Tanners' back yard, before Hurricane Katrina (above),
and after (below).

The art studio after Katrina.

More Katrina destruction.

Ouida in the backyard of her studio, with the Gulf waters
in the background. 2005

"Forever Friends"

Right: Pastor Mike Barbera
and his wife, Margaret.

Left: Tom McKenny and Dr.
Jim Tanner

Right: Tom and Jim
July 4, 2003

This was the last picture made
of Jim, two days before his
death on July 6, 2003.

Wedding Day
May 15, 2010
Bill and Ouida Sides

Fairhope, Alabama

CHAPTER 39

"OVERTOUN HOUSE"

The calendar rolled over to a new year, 2004. I had no definite plans, just struggling to get through each day and the void that Jim had left in my heart. My thoughts still clung to the past, not the future. I recalled a quote from my dear friend, Delores Winder, "Everything we go through is a lesson learned – so that other people may be helped." I had often thought that I had a story to tell; a story that might bring encouragement into the lives of others who may be experiencing similar problems (and blessings) that our family had endured. Was it possible that my story could encourage others? I began to seriously pray about it. Now, with time on my hands I timidly began writing this book.

One day, as I was writing, my phone rang. A familiar voice on the other end said, "Ouida, I want you to come to Scotland and paint some murals for us." The voice was none other than that of my dear friend, Bob Hill, missionary at Overtoun House in Dumbarton near Glasgow, Scotland. He and his wife Melissa had been in Scotland for several years, first serving in the drug infested ghetto of Glasgow, but were now heading up a ministry to unwed mothers and crisis pregnancy situations, called "A Place for Hope and Healing".

Overtoun House is an estate that was built in 1850 to resemble a castle. It was built by Lord Overtoun, a wealthy business man who was also a strong Christian. The house was dedicated to the Lord and scripture verses from the Bible were engraved over entrances into the castle, such as "Let everything that has breath, praise the Lord!"

Set on a high hill with a magnificent view of the Clydebank River, its one thousand acres were beautifully landscaped, and it even generated its own electricity, the first in the area. Inside, the house was elaborately decorated with plaster motifs, marble fireplaces, exquisite paintings of angels on the ceilings and other works of art. The Overtouns hosted many prayer meetings and Bible studies in their palatial home.

Since the castle had been dedicated to God, the Overtouns had stipulated that it must always be used in service to Him. The estate was passed on to the nephew of Lord Overtoun, since he and his wife had no children as heirs. Unable to continue the upkeep on such a grand estate the nephew had passed along the castle to the town of Dumbarton under the original terms that it must be used for God's service. It had been used in a variety of ways; a maternity hospital, a center for Wycliff Bible Translators, and even as a movie set. But the maintenance of such a grand estate was almost prohibitive for any charitable organization to keep up. And thus this abandoned and deteriorating elegant estate came to the attention of Bob and Melissa Hill.

An impossible dream? Not with God! Unwed mothers needed help. Having worked in the slum and seeing the great need among the young women who had no place to go for help, the Hills began the arduous task of getting permission from the local authorities. The town had no funds for such an undertaking, so the finances would have to come from outside sources, primarily from Christians in the United States. Bob and Melissa had been the first missionaries that the Church of the Good Shepherd had sent out; first to Japan and then to Scotland. Globe International was the main missionary agency that sponsored the Hills and were quite instrumental in this new venture. It would take a lot of money and hard physical labor to restore this most unique facility for such a ministry. But many people and many churches within and without the United States caught the vision and the massive project began.

Good Shepherd members were involved early on in the renovation process. They were about to send an additional team over for a two-week mission trip. The team consisted of about 35 people, mostly teenagers with a number of adult sponsors. Bob insisted that I be a part of the team. Me? At 72 years old? What could I do? Could I hold out? Bob was confident that I would do fine. I wished I shared his confidence.

We had to raise our own financial support and I would need a lot of art supplies for the proposed mural Bob wanted me to paint. I was surprised at how quickly the funds came in. It sounded exciting and my family was in full support of my going.

It was easy to fall in love with Scotland. As we wound our way up the rolling hillsides toward Overtoun House we were greeted with the greenest grass I had ever seen. It was the first day of June and everything was green, green. green, except for flocks of white, white sheep grazing the hills along with some very red cows. My spirit was soaring as I drank in so much color and beauty. I was actually in Scotland!

Overtoun House looked exactly like the pictures I had seen of it. Like something out of a fairy tale, its drab gray stone walls and magnificent view of Dumbarton and the Clydebank River was a story waiting to be told. Once inside, my enthusiasm waned. Despite its ornate plaster trimmings and great potential, the sheer magnitude of needed renovations was overwhelming.

The hub of the house was on the entry floor and was an L-shaped room called the Angel Room-- so called because of the absolutely gorgeous Baroque style paintings of angels on the ceilings. They had been beautifully preserved over the years despite the deterioration of the rest of the castle. There was a big problem with the room, however. At some time in the past, it had been used in movie production and the walls were painted different colors- one wall brown, one hot pink, one aqua. The fourteen foot beautiful plaster columns had been painted bright pink and trimmed in gold. It was gaudy to say the least.

Bob and Melissa were not at all happy with the décor and wondered what the team could do to help. Redecorating this room seemed to be a major priority. What about the mural I was supposed to paint? All the walls everywhere needed painting. How could I paint a mural on dirty walls? Oh, well, first things first. The huge twelve-foot roll of artist canvas we had carted from the states was placed in safe-keeping for the time being.

My mind reeled with ideas. The need was great, but where to start? There were projects going on all over the six story castle. Living quarters were provided for the missionaries and their families but there was a need for sleeping quarters for the many volunteers who were coming and going. The kitchen was not a real kitchen, but a rather large room with makeshift work spaces. It had running water, but no hot water. The furnace in the basement was not working and there was no hot water in the kitchen the entire two weeks we were there.

The need to feed about 50 people (counting staff and other volunteers) three meals a day was quite overwhelming. Because of the hard work that was required appetites were huge! Mostly, it fell on the women, but occasionally the men took turns. Food in Scotland is about two or three times as expensive as in the states. Gas, at that time was $7.85 a gallon. When we went to the grocery store it was a major ordeal, and took several cars to carry people and goods. Because food is so expensive in Scotland, the local people bought only small quantities at a time and seemed in awe at our heavily laden grocery carts. No wonder people think Americans are so rich, and in reality we are.

It was very chilly in Scotland and at the time there was very little heat in the castle; mostly we had to build fires in a huge stone fireplace on the main floor. It kept our teenage boys busy cutting wood to keep us warm. When the clothes dryer went out in the basement, we had to resort to hanging our wet clothes and towels around the giant fireplace. Imagine that with 35 plus people! Sleeping accommodations were hardly adequate and bathrooms had to be shared by many. But I, the grandmother to all, had been given the best room in the house, Esther's room. A full size bed all to myself, with windows looking out over the Clydebank River and the glorious landscape. It was too much for one person. I felt quite guilty that Esther, one of the missionaries, had given up her room for me, and even more so that others were in inadequate conditions.

But my grand suite was not to be for long. On the second day we were there a medical situation arose in which a young married couple on our team lost their first child in miscarriage. They had each been staying in the so-called "dorms" as sponsors, and I could not bear to have them apart at such a heart-breaking time. I happily gave up my room for them. Thereafter, I slept on a cot in a   hallway that offered no privacy and where I had to share a bath with 15 other people.

I never worked harder in my life or been more tired. I was in charge of painting the angel room, with for the most part inexperienced painters. Deciding on the right color was difficult, trying to match what little was left of the original paint that had the lovely name of "Water of the Nile". But we came close. And then there were the 14 foot tall plaster columns with fancy capitals at the top. We laboriously covered the hideous bright pink and gold, using a marbleizing technique which made the columns look like real marble. We used the same technique on several ornate fireplaces. Grueling work, but powerful results!

Nights are short in Scotland. It doesn't get dark until about 10:30 or 11:00 and dawn breaks around 2:30 or 3:00 AM! If you aren't careful you will work yourself to death. Many times I was on the brink of exhaustion, but we desperately wanted to finish our project. Fortunately, the Hills knew we needed a break and gave us trips to do some sight-seeing. I was most grateful to get to tour the National Gallery of Art in Edinburgh, where I saw incredible works of art; Rembrandt, Turner, John Singer Sargent, Monet, Renoir, Cezanne. What a wonderful treat! We had Fish and Chips in a Scottish pub and later visited the area around Loche Lomond. We also saw a great Scottish wedding and heard their bagpipes- all in all, a fabulous experience.

I began to realize that one of the reasons I was on this Scotland trip was to give comfort to some of the teenagers who were far from home for the first time. I became a mother to big strapping teenage boys who would come up to me and say, " Miss Ouida, I miss my mother and I need a hug". Sooner or later most everybody came down with colds and coughs. I made gallons of my hot spiced tea, loaded with citrus juices and as usual it was a cure-all.

Four days away from leaving Scotland, we still were not finished with the columns. We had lost some of our best workers due to the early return of some of our team, but the push was on. With the last ounces of our strength our goal was accomplished. The last worship service in the Angel Room with the wonderful Scottish people of the church that met at Overtoun House was an unforgettable event.

When I arrived back home I was in for a wonderful surprise. My daughter, Dawn had completely redecorated my bedroom with fresh paint, new drapes and some new furniture that had arrived in my absence. After all my hard work, what a blessing to come home to a total new look. I loved Dawn for all the labor of love she had shown me. God is so good!

CHAPTER 40

"MIRACLE ON THE WATER"

July 23, 2005 dawned bright and clear as my son Kenny my grandson Ken, Jr., and son-in-law Lewis Levy departed at 5:30 AM from Navy Point Landing in Pensacola for a day of fishing. They were scheduled to return in time for a 7:00PM twentieth birthday party for my grandson Kevin.

Debby and Lewis were on vacation from their home in South Carolina, and Dawn had joined them from Pass Christian for a few days visit with Kenny and Tammy in Cantonment, Florida. They were planning on grilling steaks for supper. Tammy talked to Kenny on his cell phone around 4:30 and he said they were heading in and should be there in an hour. Tammy wasn't worried until about 7:30 when they had not shown up or called. She tried calling on Kenny's cell and left messages. By 9:00 she was starting to really worry and called the Coast Guard to search for them.

Meanwhile, the three men, all experienced boaters and fishermen, were struggling for their lives. About 5:00 PM Kenny's twenty foot Wellcraft boat had capsized when several waves slammed into it as they were trying to free the anchor which had become lodged in some underwater wreckage. Water quickly filled the boat and as it turned upside down, the men grabbed their life jackets and put them on. The men straddled the half submerged boat and managed to cut the anchor loose. A bucket drifted by with a piece of rope attached, which they grabbed and tied to the boat and then to themselves.

Since they still had a couple of hours of sunlight, the guys figured surely they would be spotted by other boats which would be coming in, but no one saw them. As darkness set in, they found themselves drifting further and further out into the gulf until the lights on shore could no longer be seen. They had lost their cell phones and even their distress flares. It was going to be a long night. To make matters worse, a thunder storm was coming upon them, with five or six foot waves flooding over them and lightening popping all around. Kenny said it was one of the most frightening times of his life. They held hands and prayed, "God, please don't let us die out here like this." They could see sharks in the area, but also a group of porpoises that stayed near the overturned boat. God heard their cries.

Back at Kenny's house the women were beside themselves. They prayed and cried and were physically sick from worry. Tammy was in constant touch with marine authorities giving them as much information as she could think of concerning the men's plans. They did send out some search crews but could not send out search planes until daylight.

Back in Pass Christian, I knew nothing about what was going on. They did not unduly want to alarm me, hoping the men would be rescued before they had to call. At daybreak I got a call with the news. My heart almost stopped, my stomach was in knots. This involved half of the men in our family! I couldn't bear the thought of losing them. I've never prayed more fervently in my life. I began calling others to pray.

It was Sunday morning, and there would be people at Good Shepherd Church preparing for the early service. They immediately went into prayers. I called family members, friends, prayer warriors everywhere. We needed all the prayers we could get. Jason was at home with me at Merrywood, and we made the decision to go to Cantonment to be with the rest of the family. No matter the outcome, we needed each other,

Meanwhile, after surviving the miserable and frightening night, the men were exhausted and dehydrated. But daylight brought hope of being rescued. As soon as the sun rose, they went from shivering cold to scorching hot. Kenny mustarded up the courage to go underneath the boat to try to find some bottled water and perhaps a flare. When he entered the water he was nipped by several remora, a sucking type of fish that attaches itself to other fish and sharks. At first Kenny didn't know what was nipping at him and feared it could be a shark. He could not stay under water long at a time and it took him many attempts to find the cooler and locate a flare. The first flare was a dud, dashing their hopes. Eventually he found another flare and it tested positive. They would save it until they saw rescuers in view. He was also able to find two bottles of water and an orange Gatorade "That gave us more energy than you can imagine," Kenny said, "It was like we had won the lottery."

There was a remarkable miracle in their rescue. Two veteran Fish and Wildlife officers, Randy Webb and Royce Johnson, were part of the rescue team searching for the missing men. They noticed an inflated pink balloon floating on the water and wondered where it came from. About an hour later they came upon a plastic bag with several uninflated pink balloons in it. Wondering if this could be some sort of a signal or just floating debris, they radioed the information to officials on shore, who got in touch with Tammy, asking her if the men had any pink balloons with them. Tammy didn't think so, but Debby spoke up and said that Lewis sometimes kept balloons in his tackle box to use as floaters. Hope! Blessed Hope!

Randy and Royce kept following what seemed to be a current of debris and finally came upon three sets of arms waving frantically from the partially submerged vessel. They were rescued at 12:30 PM after spending roughly 21 hours adrift.

Jason and I were halfway to Pensacola when we got the call that the men had been spotted and were alive. Rescue was underway! Praise God! What joyous news! I called the church where the second service was ending and where the people received the good news with thankfulness and praise.

Jason and I arrived at Kenny's house shortly before the sunburned men did. They were exhausted and emotional as hugs and tears of joy spread amongst us. We all gave thanks for those involved in the rescue efforts.

Officials agreed that the men had done a few things right when the accident occurred. They grabbed their life-jackets, tied themselves together with rope, stayed close together and did not leave the boat. They said it is much easier to spot an overturned boat than a person in the water.

Officer Randy Webb, who is a devout Christian, summed up the rescue this way: "First it was the balloons; but we could have gone a couple of hundred yards to the right or the left and missed them. It was more than looking for a needle in a haystack. We were led to them."

CHAPTER 41

"KATRINA WAS NO LADY"

I praised God and rejoiced in his goodness for the miraculous rescue but my spirit was restless and heavy. I was unable to sleep, had lost my appetite and couldn't focus on household chores. I did a lot of praying but I didn't know exactly what to pray about. The late August heat was oppressive.

We were into the hurricane season on the Mississippi Gulf Coast. We had been through a lot of hurricanes in the thirty-three years we had lived on the Mississippi Coast and had endured some damage to our home and property during some of those storms, but for the most part the damage was minimal. In this part of the Gulf, folks always categorized the strength of a hurricane by comparing it to Hurricane Camille in 1969. Weather reports indicated that a depression was building in the Gulf waters. The Hurricane Hunters from Keesler Air Force Base in Biloxi were sent out to investigate the depression. I immediately knew this was the reason for the heaviness in my spirit.

The heat became more intense. The tropical updates reported the storm was big and still growing. People began the usual preparations: stocking up on groceries, water, flashlights, batteries, and plywood. Many did what they always did--waited until the hurricane got closer. Who knew which way it would turn? How many times had people made extensive preparations only to have the storm turn in another direction?

This time I felt the need to do more than the usual preparations. I felt inclined to pack up irreplaceable treasures, such as photographs, special pieces of jewelry, Bibles and favorite books. I also felt the need to pack some of my favorite paintings. Since my studio had not flooded during Camille I wasn't too worried about it flooding this time. Just the same, it wouldn't hurt to move some of my art work to safer places. I was especially concerned about 500 prints of my "Throne Room in Heaven" as well as the large original painting itself. Jason hauled many items up to the big house for safe-keeping.

The storm was given the name, Katrina. Updated reports on the storm showed that it was stalled about two hundred miles off shore in the Gulf of Mexico and strengthening. I finalized my plans for evacuating. I planned to travel east on Interstate 10 to Cantonment, Florida where my son Kenny and his family lived. It is a suburb of Pensacola, a little bit further north and west which was good.

Dawn and Jason decided to ride out the storm at Merrywood. It had withstood many hurricanes and I had stayed through some of them. I tried to get them to pack up and travel with me, but they declined. Jason had been through many hurricanes and had boarded up windows and doors many times only to take them down unneeded.

A report from the hurricane hunters prompted more people to take notice. One of the pilots had radioed his wife, telling her to "get out of Dodge;" he had just seen a wave about sixty feet high out in the open Gulf. I knew that the highways would be clogged with evacuation traffic so I left early on Sunday morning, around 6:30. My Ford Taurus wagon was packed to the brim. Important papers were high on the list; bank records, health records, photos, medications, a few changes of clothes. I might not need them, but I'd rather be safe than sorry. I felt terrible leaving Dawn and Jason behind, but it was their choice. If they did have to evacuate at the last minute, they could do it better without me.

The traffic wasn't bad when I started out but began to pick up as I neared the Alabama state line. I kept the car radio tuned in to the weather reports and they were increasingly ominous. I kept in touch with Dawn and Jason by cell phone. The latest reports were that the city of Pass Christian had ordered a mandatory evacuation for the areas south of the railroad tracks which included our house. Jason decided that it was indeed time to evacuate so they packed a few things quickly, including the family dog, and headed out. By this time traffic was getting quite heavy and it was difficult to make much progress on I-10. Eventually, they were able to drop down onto some county roads and make their way toward Pensacola.

I arrived at Kenny's house before noon. As dark settled in it was evident we were in for a rough night though we were 100 miles from the eye of the storm! Kenny was well prepared for the storm with ample supplies and a generator. His son, Kevin was at a friend's house across town and decided not to try to make it home, because by now the rain had begun along with thunder and lightning. The heaviness in my spirit continued unabated.

To make matters worse, a small rock band made up of some of Kevin's friends came over to Kenny's house for band practice. They didn't call ahead, they just showed up. Even though Kevin wasn't there, they decided to stay and practice anyhow. Teenagers do not seem to grasp the seriousness of violent weather. As if the sounds of the storm weren't enough, the clanging of the musical instruments, especially the drums, added to the bedlam. My head was splitting, my nerves were shot. Finally, they left and things seemed to calm down a little.

It was quite late when Dawn and Jason got in. By now Kenny's house had lost power and with it our link to what was happening on the Mississippi Coast. He hooked up the portable generator. Radio reports were sporadic. We could hear and feel tree limbs banging on the house, a fearsome sound. I had elected to sleep on Kenny's living room sofa, although sleep escaped me. Eventually, I drifted into a fitful sleep. I woke up and my head was killing me, I felt nauseated and there was a strong smell in the room. Gas fumes!

I stumbled into Kenny and Tammy's room. Immediately, Kenny took charge of the matter. He had set the generator outside of the house on the sun-deck and had propped a piece of plywood over it to keep the rain off of it.. He did not realize that the plywood forced the fumes into the house through cracks around the door next to it. Not only that, but the heat from the generator had actually begun to burn the wooden siding on the outside of the house. Only the rain kept it from catching into a full blown blaze. I felt quite sick from the fumes and could not get back to sleep. The storm was raging full force outside as were my emotions on the inside. There was little sleep for any of us that awful night. As daylight dawned we saw that Kenny's yard had been hard hit, with tree damage and limbs on the house. Waiting for news was agonizing, but nothing could be done about it. We were dry, we had food and we had each other, thank God. How grateful I was that Dawn and Jason had evacuated to Kenny's house.

When the electric power was finally restored to Kenny's house, we were able to get more news about the hurricane's destruction. In New Orleans, some 200 miles away, they were dealing with problems of broken levees and massive flooding, especially in the city's Ninth Ward. The images were horrible and consumed most of the national news coverage.

The eye of the hurricane had only brushed New Orleans. Landfall was in Waveland and Bay St. Louis, Mississippi. The storm was so huge that it covered almost the entire Gulf of Mexico. It knocked out two major bridges connecting the central coastline of Mississippi with the rest of the state, creating havoc with travel and rescue efforts. It was much worse than Camille had been in 1969.

CHAPTER 42

"THE AFTERMATH"

The deadly storm's hurricane force winds began around 2:00 AM August 29 in Mississippi. Landfall couldn't have come at a worse time, around 4:30 AM with high-tide due to arrive around 8:00AM. The storm surge in the Bay of St. Louis, just west of Pass Christian, was later determined to be at 28 feet, causing massive flooding over about 90% of the coastline. This incredible storm surge pushed water into local bayous, rivers and streams carrying the flooding inland as much as six to twelve miles. In some areas the flood waters covered some portions of heavily traveled Interstate 10. There were reports that the rain lasted 17 hours and spawned as many as 11 tornadoes.

The reports trickling in were traumatizing. Authorities were warning people to stay away and not to return to check on loved ones or properties. It was too dangerous. Power lines and trees were down on many, many roads and there was widespread flooding. Utter chaos everywhere. Only emergency crews and first responders were allowed in. The National Guard was activated.

Quite naturally, we were anxious to get back to the Pass but were trying to abide by the advice of the authorities. It was hard to restrain Kenny and

Jason. Into the chaos they felt they must go. Kenny loaded up a chainsaw, the generator, and other supplies. Dawn went with them. They would not allow me to go.

Traveling on I-10 as much as they could, they eventually had to take back roads due to traffic jams and washed out bridges. When at last they reached Pass Christian, they were forbidden to drive south of the railroad tracks even though Dawn and Jason both had valid licenses showing they lived in the very area. They knew back roads though and managed to sneak through. Kenny found it almost impossible to navigate Second Street, our street. There were houses in the middle of almost every side street and no people could be seen anywhere. Finally, as Merrywood came into view there were shouts of joy and praise to God for his divine protection over our home. Proudly she stood, a sentinel among the rubble.

God, indeed, had supernaturally protected our beloved home. While there appeared to be no serious structural damage, there was minor roof damage from tree branches, but there did not even appear to be a broken window! Unbelievable! The studio was another story. It had been knocked off its foundation on the front part of the building. The front porch had been heavily damaged, with the large wooden and brick columns torn away, the brick steps no longer in place. The front door had blown off its hinges and windows were broken. Inside the main room of the house, it looked like a giant blender had taken everything and scrambled it into oblivion. Water marks inside the room showed that the water had been at least 3 to 4 feet high. Dirty, debris filled water had left its ugly scars behind. Paintings, art supplies, easels, books, were a colossal mess.

The guest house, which was home for Dawn, did not fare well either. Severe roof damage, broken windows, but amazingly, there was no flooding inside. The water had come right up to the front porch stoop, but had not entered the little cottage. When I finally saw it for myself weeks later, I could only think of the scripture in the book of Job in the Bible where it says, "Who shut up the sea behind doors, when it burst forth from the womb, when I made the clouds its garment and wrapped it in thick darkness, and when I fixed limits for it, and set its doors and bars in place, and when I said, "THIS FAR YOU MAY COME AND NO FARTHER, HERE

IS WHERE YOUR PROUD WAVES STOP!". Job 38:8-11.

Dawn said that first night after the storm was very dark and very quiet. They watched the remains of a nearby apartment complex burn to the ground for several hours. There was no help to send or need to send it. After surveying the situation and being quite overwhelmed by the sheer magnitude of the devastation, the little crew of Kenny, Jason and Dawn realized there was very little they could do.

The next morning the street in front of the house was filled with vehicle after vehicle of first responders. Police, electricians, firemen, men in hardhats with pickup trucks; dozens and dozens from many states, were slowly picking their way down the debris strewn street to set up a staging area in the Walmart parking lot. Walmart faced the Gulf on Highway 90 and it's property adjoined mine. Normally the store could not be seen from my house because of the wooded area and thick foliage between the two properties. Now, however, the trees had mostly been stripped away exposing the blown out Walmart store with all its contents strewn all across my backyard and the beach. Clothing and merchandise were dangling from the damaged trees and the stench from rotting food permeated the hot, humid air.

Every morning we had always put out a large American flag on the front porch so that's what Dawn did. She put the flag in its holder and began to sweep the porch. It wasn't long before a reporter from Pensacola, Florida approached her. Placing the flag in its holder had deeply moved the first responders. When asked who lived in the house, she replied it was the Tanner home.

The reporter replied, "I just did a news story about some Tanners who had a boating accident off the coast of Florida." And to the surprise of everyone, Dawn said, "That was my brother, my nephew, and my brother-in-law!"

Coincidence? It was a divine appointment!

Merrywood had no electricity, no water, no phone and the heat was unbearable. The kids cleaned out the refrigerator and freezer and decided to return to Pensacola.

When they arrived back in Pensacola, I could tell by their faces that they had seen and experienced horrendous trauma. They were solemn and weary, unlike their usual jovial natures. One thing they were adamant about, they did not want me to return to Pass Christian anytime in the foreseeable future. After a family conference, we decided that Dawn would drive me to Debby and Lewis's house in South Carolina. I was still battling high blood pressure and now depression. They wanted me to get away from devastation and misery. That was fine with me.

Kenny and Jason made plans to go back to the coast better prepared. They scurried around buying gas cans, generators, chainsaws, and all the fuel they could get their hands on to take back to Mississippi. Supplies were in short supply everywhere-- and virtually non-existent along coastal Mississippi. The needs were staggering.

Chapter 43
"South Carolina – My Interim Home"

My station wagon was still packed with the belongings I had taken from Merrywood. Five days after Katrina, Dawn and I started the long drive to South Carolina, passing caravans of rescue units and power trucks heading south. What a welcome sight to know where they were headed. But others, like ourselves, were heading to points north and east, their belongs tied to their vehicles, going to who knew where.

It was great to be at Debby's and Lewis' tranquil country home How I needed the reprieve. My sincere and fervent prayers went out for all who had suffered from the storm. I longed to do more though. With so many cell phone towers destroyed across several states I used my computer and soon developed a relay station of sorts. I was able to keep informed as well as inform others.

I found out through my communication system that thirty-five families from the Church of the Good Shepherd had suffered terrible losses. This was very upsetting to me. I wanted to be there for them. I felt my blood pressure rising and depression enveloped me. I was having difficulty eating and sleeping. Debby made an appointment to see her doctor, who was kind and understanding and provided the medical help I needed.

After a week, Dawn was anxious to get back to Pass Christian and help Jason, but had no transportation. We had driven my vehicle, and I would need it while in South Carolina and to get back home. She had been wanting to get a small pickup truck for herself and we worked out the finances. God did the rest. He led us to a parking lot of used cars and the exact pickup she wanted. It even had a fish symbol on the back. We knew that was God's stamp of approval. She was soon on her way.

Debby and Lewis were also anxious to get down to the coast to see the damage for themselves. They left about a week after Dawn and I was left alone at their house except for the companionship of their Labrador retriever, Black Bart. I felt very well protected. When they returned they recommended that I not go back for a good while. They, too, had been overwhelmed at the damage and destruction they had seen.

Whenever I ventured out to a supermarket or shopping center people were putting together trailer loads of supplies to send to the stricken areas of the coast. When people realized I was a hurricane survivor, they were kind and helpful, even inviting me into their homes for meals and calling to check on me.

Weeks passed and I was content to man my station at the computer and spend time with Debby, One day I got some pictures that sent me back to the doctor's office. The pictures were of an open grave, an empty grave filled with water. My heart went out to Lewis The grave belonged to his mother: Phyllis Levy, my friend, neighbor, and fellow in-law. She had been laid to rest that May, less than four months before Katrina, in the same cemetery where Jim was buried. Live Oak Cemetery is in a low-lying area of town, not far from the beach. Many of the newer graves had been unearthed by the storms raging fury. My soul grieved.

A few yards from her empty grave was Jim's simple grave marker, undisturbed. He rested peacefully.

CHAPTER 44

"MERRYWOOD – STILL HOME"

While Dawn and I were in South Carolina Jason was living back at Merrywood, along with his friend Steve, whose Pass Christian home had been destroyed by the storm. They carried water from a neighbor's swimming pool to flush toilets and bathed with an outdoor camp shower. The heat was merciless and the stench of debris and rotting food from Wal-Mart unbearable. Added to the misery were hordes of mosquitoes breeding in the areas where water still lingered.

By this time first responders were on the scene in great numbers. Among them were dozens of Amish and Mennonite men and women, many from Lancaster County in Pennsylvania. They were among the first to tackle the tree problems on our property. Our beautiful back yard was hardly recognizable, huge oak trees down, smaller trees on the guest cottage and the master bath in the big house. Broken lattice fences and limbs littered the yard. These wonderful volunteers made quick work of clearing the back yard and then began working on the studio grounds, which had lost nearly all its trees.

Jason and Steve were working alongside the volunteers. Kenny had come back over from Pensacola to help as well. Before his return trip to the coast, Kenny had gone to a bakery in Pensacola to buy bread to take to Mississippi and the bakery had filled his van full of bread at no charge. What a blessing that turned out to be. People and relief agencies were beginning to respond to the dire needs and supplies began to flow into the stricken area, along with more volunteers.

The need for fresh food was a great priority at this time. Many of the volunteers provided their own food, and the Salvation Army and other agencies were doing their best to meet the needs, but the situation was critical. Early on after the storm, a wonderful Christian man anticipated the need and came from Kentucky in a pick-up with a portable grill. He set up a make-shift kitchen on the beach in Pass Christian. Greg Porter would go on to play a significant role in the recovery efforts by feeding literally thousands of people in the months to come.

When the tantalizing smell of grilled hamburgers wafted along the debris strewn beach, it seemed people came out of the woodwork.. The need was so great that Greg had to call in reinforcements and soon a tent was set up on a vacant lot on the east end of Pass Christian, near the Wal-Mart area. Over time, another larger tent with a red-and-white striped top was set up and given the unforgettable name of God's Katrina Kitchen. This wonderful feeding station would go on to provide much more than physical food; it would become a healing place for broken spirits, shattered lives and the beginning of hopes restored.

For me personally, the tent would begin a healing process after the trauma of the worst natural disaster I had ever experienced.

Chapter 45
"Nothing Would Ever be the Same"

I thought I was prepared to face the reality of Katrina's wrath. After all, I'd had over a month to sift through news reports, photos, phone calls and e-mails detailing the staggering aftermath of the storm's ferocious attack on the coastal areas of the Gulf of Mexico. But while driving back from South Carolina I was appalled at the wind damage even two hundred miles away from Pass Christian. Trees were hardest hit and many roof-tops were covered with blue tarps, provided by FEMA.

The closer I got to the coast of Mississippi the worse things looked. What was once a lovely drive along Highway 49 from Hattiesburg now looked like war-torn terrain. My stomach began to feel the now familiar churning of the past few weeks.

I took the back roads, knowing it would be difficult to get through the more heavily traveled ones. It was extremely gratifying to see so many rescue units headed toward the gulf coast; lots of electrical crews from far away states, van loads of volunteer workers, trucks loaded with food and supplies. My heart was warmed when I saw Operation Blessing trucks, as well as Samaritan's Purse semi-tractor trucks headed south. I gave them all big "thumbs up" signs each time I passed. My heart was flooded with gratitude toward all who were giving of their time and resources to help-the Body of Christ in action.

I had been forewarned that National Guard troops remained stationed at all the railroad crossings into Pass Christian to keep unauthorized persons from entering the town and to deter looters who swooped in like vultures even the day after the storm. The guardsman accepted my credentials (driver's license) and let me pass onto a city street. I made my way to Second Street, my street. Or was it? What happened to the Longwood Apartments? Piles of rubble and debris lined both sides of the street. Things looked somewhat familiar but I couldn't be sure. But then, up ahead, yes! There on the left was my beloved Merrywood! Almost as stately as ever. I could only think of one word, beacon! She was a beacon of light and hope amid a sea of chaos.

She appeared almost unscathed. Out front swaying gently in the breeze was our flag, Old Glory! I had seen hundreds of American flags on my trip back home; a symbol of the fighting spirit, the can do attitude of America's greatness.

Home! I was home again, but as I was soon to discover, THINGS WOULD NEVER BE THE SAME AGAIN.

CHAPTER 46

"REALITY SETS IN"

Dawn had tried to prepare me ahead of time for what I would be facing when I returned home, but in my wildest imagination I could never have foreseen the sheer magnitude of Katrina's destruction. My house, my street and parts of the neighborhood had escaped the brunt of the wrath, but not so only a few hundred yards away. Gone was almost the entire street to the west of our house, including the house of some close friends, Dick and Freda Oden. They were in their mid-seventies and homeless with nothing more than the clothes on their backs. They needed a place to stay while they applied for a FEMA trailer, and we were glad to provide a bedroom for them.

Dawn took me for a drive the first day I was back. It was more like traversing a hazardous trail. Much of Highway 90 along the beach was almost impassable, with huge chunks of concrete broken and stacked against each other. Gone were whole rows of condos and apartments, restaurants, and beautiful homes. The once showplace Scenic Drive could not be navigated by car. Huge mansions, gone. Majestic live oak trees that had stood for hundreds of years, now ravaged with broken limbs, stripped of their leaves and Spanish moss and littered with ghost-like shreds of clothing, eerie survivors of the storm.

I grew very quiet. I felt as though my heart would burst from the sadness I was experiencing. I knew most of the people who had lived in those houses and condos. Where were they now? On and on it went, miles of destruction, driveways leading nowhere. I could not recognize where I was at times. The town's stop lights and most of the street signs - gone.

Slowly we inched our way toward downtown; the harbor, devastated. Yacht Club, gone. Post Office, gone. My bank, gone. Where was the vault that held my important papers? The grocery store, city hall, the library, the police station . . . .all gone. The high school where my son graduated, gone. The beautiful Trinity Episcopal Church, destroyed by Camille then rebuilt, now destroyed again. And there behind the church, the old Live Oak Cemetery - head stones broken and turned over, trees broken or stripped bare. I searched and found what I was eager to see, Jim Tanner's grave marker, untouched. It was what he had requested, simple and small. Now I knew why he had been so insistent on no big headstone.

There only fifty or so feet away was an open grave filled with water--- Lewis' mother's grave. The vast reality of the storm's wrath hit me. Where was she? Would she ever be found? How many more situations like this could there be?

We gingerly wound our way back down Second Street. The once beautiful city park with its massive live oak trees, though, battered, held a sense of normality about it. It was one of the first things in the city to receive restoration in a city that needed a place of peace, rest, and safety. This restoration was due in large part to the efforts of Robin Roberts of Good Morning America fame. Pass Christian was her hometown. She had graduated from its high school. Her family were outstanding citizens and greatly respected. She had brought in television crews to report on the damage and lend support toward the park's restoration. She got wonderful results and it lifted the spirits of all the town folk.

Back at my house I wandered through my lovely living room, where not a picture hung crooked on the walls; into the dining room where my beautiful china and crystal remained undisturbed. It was though in my own home, the storm had never even happened. I sat down and began to weep. I was overcome by feelings of guilt. Why me? Why, oh Lord, did You spare my home in almost pristine condition, when outside and all around there was such massive destruction?

In my heart I knew why. When we moved into Merrywood in 1972, we dedicated the house to God. We endeavored to use it for His glory. Still it was overwhelming that God was so merciful in allowing us this sanctuary "for such a time as this". He knew what we didn't, that we would again be using it for His glory; to house the homeless, the volunteers, to host the many friends who needed to come to a familiar place that seemed "normal", peaceful and comfortable.

Thus began the long line of volunteers, friends who had lost their homes, and others who needed temporary lodging during this time.

CHAPTER 47

"GOD'S KATRINA KITCHEN"

I visited the feeding tent that became known as God's Katrina Kitchen the first night I was back home. Dawn suggested that we go there to eat. Frankly there was no place else to eat, unless I cooked and I was in no mood to do so. I felt guilty eating there when I had a kitchen at home, but I quickly learned that the volunteers were not just dishing up comfort food, but comfort itself.

With warm greetings of "God bless you" and love in their hearts, these servants of the Lord were beginning a healing and restoration of hope within those of us hurting so badly. The tent served three hot meals a day, beginning with a hearty breakfast for the many volunteers as well as locals who were in need. The meals were free of charge to all, but donations were gladly accepted and God continually supplied the food. In the beginning the tent served dozens of people daily which soon grew to hundreds.

I looked forward to my nightly visits to the tent always abuzz with people. Locals came not only to eat but to connect with one another. Communication lines were still down so the tent served as contact point for the community. Notes were posted on a bulletin board where people could

213

leave or receive messages. People were reunited with friends and loved ones with whom they had lost touch.

Volunteers flowed into the coastal area from all over the country. Among them were many Mennonites and Amish people. I had never been around these wonderful people before, but found them to be some of the most loving and helpful I had ever met. The women worked as hard as the men with the cleanup in addition to doing much of the food preparation. We loved it when fresh recruits came in from Lancaster County bringing with them home-made pies. I had my first taste of "shoo-fly-pie"- yummy!

The tent provided not only physical food, but spiritual food as well. Nightly worship began taking place with great preaching, testimonies, and music. The services were spearheaded by a missionary evangelist from Georgia, David Roper. He had come soon after the hurricane to do what he could and God had used him in countless ways- from dishing up food to leading the worship services and praying with the people. When Greg Porter, who started the kitchen had to be out of town, Pastor Dave as he came to be known, was the man in charge.

As volunteers and locals sat at long tables eating together, many friendships were formed. Volunteers listened with interest and compassion as survivors related their stories. I became good friends of some people from a church in Boston. When they learned I was an artist and had lost my studio, they invited me to exhibit a painting in their church-sponsored art show for Black History Month there. Some volunteers from Connecticut became interested in my art work and actually purchased a couple of paintings from me. Often I was asked to share my story about the survival of my house with the people who were in the evening services at the tent.

A lot of young teenagers volunteered at the tent and help clean out the muddy houses. They slept in pup tents, using portable toilets and makeshift showers. The heat was unbearable with no air-conditioning to be had. I felt sorry for some of the young girls and found it lifted their spirits if I invited them to my house for a real tub bath and hot tea out of a china cup.

My house was usually filled to capacity with either locals or volunteers. I really enjoyed getting to know the Amish and Mennonites. I had the idea that they were more or less "stuffy" or rigid in their faith, but they were delightful and lots of fun. Even after long days of extremely hard work, they would bring out their music instruments and sing, but were up with the sun the next morning. One of my great delights is to still keep in touch with some of these great friends.

One day while cleaning the grounds around my studio, a young Amish man came across a Bible laying on a pile of debris and asked me what he should do with it. He surely did not want to throw away a Bible even if it had been water-logged. When he brought it to me, I looked at the name in the front. I realized it belonged to the son of our church secretary. How did it get in my yard? The family had lived in some apartments down the street from me many years before, but surely they would have not knowingly left the Bible behind. I took the Bible to the church. Ava was delighted to get it and called her son who then was living in Texas. How it came to be where it was found remains a mystery

Another "Bible" story happened early after the storm. Jason's friend, Steve, was cleaning up around his parents' home on the bay-front in Pass Christian, when he found a Bible laying on the outside deck. It was opened to the first chapter of Proverbs and his eyes fell on these words beginning with verse 25, "Since you ignored all my advice and would not accept my rebuke, (vs. 26) I in turn will laugh at your disaster; I will mock when calamity overtakes you- (vs.27) when calamity overtakes you like a storm, when disaster sweeps over you like a whirlwind; when distress and trouble overwhelm you...." (vs.33) "But whoever listens to me will live in safety and be at ease, without fear of harm." (NIV)

There are countless stories of unusual happenings during those recovery days. Recovery of lost articles was high on the list. One lady who lost her entire house down to the slab found her deceased husband's watch in the exact spot where his nightstand used to be. She bemoaned losing a favorite pair of scissors only later to find them imbedded in a flower bed. God is the God of the little things as well as the big.

On a personal note: I found an antique framed mirror that had been on the wall of my studio unbroken under a huge pile of rubble. A favorite water-color painting of a magnolia that was not under glass or protected in any way, survived the flood inside my studio. I have much for which to be thankful.

CHAPTER 48

"BEAUTY IN THE ASHES"

A strange phenomenon happened in the Pass Christian area within weeks of Katrina. Sunflowers began popping up all over the place, hundreds and hundreds of them, along roadways, in vacant lots, around empty house slabs, and in the woods. Along the road next to my house an enormous sunflower sprouted up. It was dinner-plate in size and perfectly formed. I wanted to pick it but hated to stop its growth. I wanted to see just how big it would get. Just when I decided to pick it, I found someone had beat me to it.

Where were all these beautiful flowers coming from? Seeds from the Walmart store? Bird-feeders? People's yards? God knew we needed a touch of beauty to gladden our spirits, a promise of brighter days to come. I, for one, was very thankful for the sight, and especially when I found my own special sunflower blessing in the backyard of my dilapidated studio. A glimmer of bright yellow caught my attention. Upon investigation I discovered a sunflower stalk taller than my head that was covered with thirty-three blooms! Thirty-three blooms? The number of years of our Lord's earthly life! Another sign from God! Beauty for my eyes, to gladden my heart, to lift my spirit! Dawn and I made pictures.

216

I felt compelled to do a painting of the sunflower bush. Soon after, news came that the Mississippi Museum of Art in Jackson was hosting an exhibit of "Katrina Art", paintings that had been done by coastal artists since the hurricane. It provided an opportunity to showcase art done after the storm since there was no other venue for exhibiting on the coast.

I decided to enter my sunflower painting and another painting that I had recently done. From an upstairs window I was surveying my backyard and damaged studio when the thought came to me, "I have before and after pictures of the studio, but I wonder what it must have looked like during the storm". I began to picture in my mind what it might have been like. Using an old photo of the studio, I laid in the basics and then began painting in the wind and the rain, trees blowing and falling on the roof, water rising and entering the building. It was an emotional moment for me. I could imagine the water crashing into the windows, the door being blown off its hinges letting the black swirling water inside covering the floors, furniture, irreplaceable art works and thousands of dollars' worth of art supplies. The sounds must have been terrifying, thunder, winds screaming, lightening crashing, things breaking, the awful smells. It all came rushing into my emotions like the flood itself. Afterwards, I was physically spent. I entered both paintings in the Jackson show. Our local newspaper did a full page article on my paintings complete with photos.

CHAPTER 49

"MY CHURCH FAMILY"

My first Sunday back at Good Shepherd was an emotional one. Services were held on the concrete slab foundation with the hot sun bearing down on us. Off to the side of the foundation stood the once beautiful white baby-grand piano, now ruined from the rain and debris. Missing were the stained glass windows we had painstakingly made ourselves. But miracle of miracles, they had been boarded up by Pastor Mike Cassagne and all had survived! Apparently a tornado had struck the sanctuary-the walls fell outward, but the stained glass windows stood! Praise God!

It was wonderful seeing the church, the body of Christ, rallying and worshiping together. Tears of joy and tears of sadness flowed. There were testimonies from those who had survived tremendous losses as well as miraculous recoveries. Though many families had been forced to leave the area, worshiping along with us was a host of volunteers, including the Amish and Mennonites. In fact, our church became a temporary headquarters for some of the volunteers, who slept in the Sunday school rooms and used our kitchen facilities which had not sustained damage. Our bond with these loving and hardworking people grew stronger each day.

My heart was heavy for my suffering church family and other beloved friends who lived along the coast. Tom and Marty McKenney had built a lovely retirement home in Ocean Springs. Their son, Jeff, had built a home next door to his and both homes were totally destroyed. Their daughters' homes, Susan's in Ocean Springs and Melissa's in Long Beach, had both been heavily damaged.   I grieved deeply for my friends' losses, feeling guilty that I was living comfortably in my lovely home that had barely been scratched. Reports reached me that many of my artist friends had lost their studios, art supplies and valuable art works.   To this I could relate.

My grandson, Jason was working with the Passport office in downtown New Orleans before the storm. It was weeks before he was able to make the daily commute to work. Confronting him on both sides of the interstate were miles of flooded homes and shopping centers. I was so glad that when Jason finally got home each day, he found refuge in our beloved Merrywood. We had shelter, food, air conditioning and above all, each other.

Slowly, some semblance of normalcy returned to our little town. Daily, truckloads of debris were hauled away to landfills; city offices were set up in double-wide trailers. The local library reopened in trailers and books poured in from everywhere. President George W. Bush and Laura made several appearances in the area to offer support and encouragement. Laura was especially involved in the restoration of the local schools, making extra trips on her own.

FEMA was much involved in the recovery process as well. A large feeding tent was set up in the central part of town. Their facility was better than God's Katrina Kitchen and even had its own form of make-shift air-conditioning. The meals were excellent but sadly there was something lacking in their efforts. That something was the genuine love and compassion, the spiritual influence that was evident at God's Katrina Kitchen. Still, a lot of needs were met and we were grateful that our government provided so well for us.

Back in my own house, in my own room in the wee hours of the night, I lay awake thinking, praying, grieving, sometimes crying. It all seemed like an unholy night-mare. While in my own home things were relatively normal, I had only to step outside my doors for reality to set in. Destruction, despair, desolation in every direction. No beauty anywhere except for the now peaceful and beautiful waters of the Gulf, its sunrises and sunsets, reminders that God was still with us, still on His throne.

CHAPTER 50

"WHAT NOW?"

When infrastructure is knocked out, the trek back to normal is slow. Pass Christian's business district was almost totally destroyed. The local post office was functioning in several mobile trailers north of town. Schools also were meeting in trailers. There were no grocery stores, no drug stores or restaurants. We were told that it would take about seven years for the area to recover from Katrina.

Along with the inconveniences, we were experiencing the ugliness of destroyed homes and businesses. It was sad to see the scars and gaping holes in the landscape from the many live oaks, hundreds of years old, now completely uprooted. There was no beauty to be seen except as I had mentioned before, in God's creation of sea and skies.

While I was one of the most blessed survivors on the coast (with regards to my home), at times I realized that I, too, had suffered significant losses. While my house had sustained relatively minor damage, I still had roof leaks, the loss of front and backyard lattice fences, trees and foliage damage etc. Painfully significant was the loss of my wonderful art studio, all of my expensive artist materials and volumes of irreplaceable art works. Lost also, was the small guest house in the backyard, which was home to

221

my daughter, Dawn, and all her earthly possessions, including her personal piano. All of this was going to take a lot of money and a lot of work.

We had been told, even by an insurance agent that we did not need to carry flood insurance because no flood waters had ever reached as far inland as our property. We did of course carry wind insurance but most of our damage had been from flood waters. The debris from the Walmart store was strewn all around us. The once lovely woods around us were now littered with articles of clothing, thousands of plastic Walmart bags, and assorted damaged merchandised. The stench of rotting food still lingered in the air weeks after the storm had passed.

I had often wondered if I would be able to continue living at Merrywood after Jim died. The house was paid for, but the taxes, insurance and maintenance were a serious concern for me. Jim and I had discussed the possibility of downsizing but never gave it much consideration. Now, what should I do?

I needed to hear from God. Oh, how I needed to hear from Him. Should I sell the house? If so, who would buy it? Where would I move to? The entire Mississippi coast had been devastated.

And then one day a letter came in the mail. A letter with an offer to buy my house. It was from a local realtor but offered no specific information. Was this somehow of God? Was He setting something in motion in answer to my prayers? After some time of reflection I decided to contact the realtor.

The picture was changing. The offer was no ordinary real estate deal. It seemed that the city officials had been in contact with the Walmart headquarters as to the possibility of the rebuilding of their store in the same location, with one exception- they needed more space, further inland. In essence, they needed my property and that of my surrounding neighbors in order to rebuild. Pass Christian was desperate to have a big tax base business in the city. It could be a win/win situation.

One might think that I would jump at such an offer. But it was not that easy. I was under considerable pressure from the realtor as well as the city officials to keep my price low else Walmart might relocate in another area outside the city limits. If I refused to sell would I be ruling out my neighbors chances to sell? I attended several meetings of the local planning committee on restoration and was informed that the surrounding property was to be zoned commercial. Now what?

The hardest part of all, could I bear to part with my beloved Merrywood? The house that had been home to the Tanner family for 33 years; where prayer meetings and Bible studies were held every Thursday night for 23 years? The birth-place of the Church of the Good Shepherd, weddings and receptions, Christmas parties and 4th of July picnics, family reunions and grandchildren playing in the secret stairway- the memories were overwhelming.

What would become of Merrywood if I sold? I couldn't bear the thought of it being torn down. Not only because of its historical significance, but because of its architectural value. Sure it needed some work but it had good bones. Excellent materials and workmanship had gone into it. It was built to last. Last, it must.

As I pondered all these things in my heart, the words in Proverbs 11:14 came to mind, "Where no counsel is, the people fall: but in the multitude of counselors there is safety." I began to seek out trusted counselors, starting with my family, pastors, close friends, my lawyer. All agreed that to secure my future and to make a fresh start after Katrina, I should sell--with one exception, Merrywood could not be torn down.

During this time of indecision I had another very heavy burden on my heart. My only brother, Leslie Trigg, was dying of prostate cancer. He lived in my home town of Waynesboro, Mississippi, 135 miles away. When first diagnosed he was given two years to live but the cancer progressed rapidly and we realized we were looking at months or even weeks. I greatly valued my brother's business advice and when he learned of the potential sale he advised me to go for it. Sadly, he did not live to see the sale come to pass, but he died knowing I would be well provided for.

My world was rapidly changing, In two years I had lost my husband, my brother, my town, my art studio, so many friends and neighbors, a damaged church. It was hard to bear, but I had much to be thankful for, indeed, I counted my many blessings. Now, the choice was mine.

If I could have seen into the future I would never have worried about Merrywood at all. God had plans for it beyond my imagination!

CHAPTER 51
"TO EVERYTHING THERE IS A SEASON"

It was settled. Merrywood would be sold with the provision that it could not be torn down. Dawn and Jason wanted to stay on the coast but I wanted to get away from the destruction. I wanted to see beauty.

I remembered visiting the lovely little town of Fairhope, Alabama on several occasions. Jim and I had also mentioned the possibility of retiring there at one time. Fairhope is a small, quaint town on the eastern shore of Mobile Bay. Known for its abundance of flowers in the downtown area, as well as its art festivals, it loomed as an oasis for me. Another thing that appealed to me was that an old and very dear friend of mine was now living there. Nadine Fowler had been my prayer partner for many years on the Mississippi coast. We used to walk the sandy beaches of Pass Christian and write scriptures in the sand as we prayed and worshiped the Lord.

I made contact with Nadine who warmly welcomed me to visit her and check out the possibility of moving to the area. I found out that Mobile Bay was once known as the Bay of the Holy Spirit. Was this a sign from God?

Fairhope was appealing indeed, even its name. I felt my spirit begin to heal as I toured the tree-lined streets and had lunch in one of the quaint restaurants, Nadine hosted me and advised me as to available housing.

I had once told Jim that I would like to live in a brand new house before I died. One that was built to look old, but had modern conveniences and was energy efficient. This was my chance. Fairhope was experiencing a housing boom, because of so many people re-locating due to the hurricane. There were lovely homes to be had, but the prices had gone way up. I had intended to downsize, but was not happy with what I saw I ended up having a medium sized home built that met most of my needs, including a one-room art studio.

It was exciting being able to select things like flooring, light fixtures, paint and a few new pieces of furniture. I made the 100 mile trip to Fairhope quite often during the building process. Each time I returned to Merrywood, my stomach churned. I questioned my decision to relocate. Was I really hearing from God? Daily I prayed for guidance. One day I felt the Holy Spirit saying to me, "If you asked me for direction, why do you question every decision you make?"

Why indeed, did I question every decision, causing more stress for myself? If I felt alright when I made a decision, why not leave it at that. I needed to trust God to block anything that was not from Him and give myself peace of mind.

Remembering my widowhood, I took comfort in God's word in Isaiah 54:5 which says, "For your Maker is your husband-the Lord Almighty is His name..." Had He not already provided for me in so many ways? He was and is a faithful provider,

CHAPTER 52
"A TIME TO WEEP, A TIME TO LAUGH"

Merrywood was beloved by many, many people, especially those who had attended the Thursday night meetings. To honor their attachment to the house and the memory of those special prayer meetings, I thought it would be nice to have a final "farewell" before I had to vacate the house.

I sent out letters to as many as I had addresses for, inviting them to join us for a 3-night series of meetings at Merrywood. I planned three nights so that any who could not make it on a Thursday night, could come on another. The event was held in early May of 2007 since the prayer meeting began May 5, 1973.

What a joy to see old friends, to praise and worship the Lord and fellowship together. David Gervais came from his home in Citronelle, Alabama to play the piano. Tom McKenney taught from God's Word and as usual we ended the evening with a special time of prayer.

It was bitter-sweet. The end of an era, but a foretaste of Heavenly things to come.

Despite my protesting the church planned a big farewell party for me. I didn't want the fanfare. So many had lost so much, had moved away and no party had been given to honor them. I was embarrassed to be singled out for such an event. But my pastors and friends would have it no other way. Because the church had begun in Merrywood, we were considered among the founders. Therefore, we should have a party, and what a party it was! The setting was the church backyard where white tents had been set up. Magnolias, were everywhere, from the paper-plates and napkins to the beautiful cake. Food was abundant, as were wonderful friends. Many volunteers who were still helping out after Katrina were present, including the Amish and Mennonites whom I had grown to love.

Following the meal, we assembled in the newly repaired sanctuary, and I was presented with the most unusual gift anyone ever received. I have mentioned before that the church members had made our own stained glass windows which had survived the hurricane. Now, one of them was going to Fairhope with me. For once in my life, my motor-mouth was speechless! What an incredible gesture! I was emotionally overcome. The window, standing eight feet tall, bore the emblem of a standing lamb, representing of course, the Good Shepherd, the Lamb of God. What does one say or do in light of such a priceless gift! A part of the church was moving with me! To God be the Glory!

Back at Merrywood, it was time to move on, the end of an era. How do you pack up thirty-five years of memories? It was difficult and sad. My good friend, Brenda Rolison, spent hours helping me pack. The day came to sweep out the house and give up the key--the day I had been dreading most of all. I stood by the fireplace and looked toward the dining room – now totally empty. I could almost hear voices chattering, singing, laughter ringing. My heart was pierced through with sadness. Brenda was there to cry along with me.

I had hoped my new house in Fairhope would be ready to move in by June 8, which would be my son Kenny's 50th birthday. What a great way to christen a new house! And it came to pass! On June 6th, the movers arrived and all the family and a few friends made fast work of setting things in order. We ended one era with a party and began another. It eased the transition..

It was good to see beauty again. Fairhope had much to offer. As soon as possible I began to explore the neighborhood. To my delight, I discovered a huge field of sunflowers only a couple of blocks away. In the opposite direction I drove through a grove of ancient live-oak trees that made a tunnel of leaves and limbs over the road. Fairhope sits on the high banks of Mobile Bay and the town "square" is actually a park by the bay, complete with a rose garden, a large flowing fountain and a pier reaching out a quarter of a mile into the bay waters. So many things about the area reminded me of Pass Christian; the water, the small-town feel, lovely homes and lots of trees. I was beginning to feel at home.

Nadine was great in helping me fit in. I began attending church with her and she helped me find new doctors, shopping centers, anything I could possibly need. Everything was so convenient. After living in ravaged post-Katrina coastal areas, convenience was a welcome thing.

Not long after I had moved, I received a phone call from my artist friend, Alan Flattmann. He told me that he was going to Italy to do a workshop. Would I like to go? Would I ever! The workshop would primarily be taught in Tuscany, a painter's paradise! There would be the opportunity to extend the trip and see Rome, the Sistine Chapel, and other points of interest. I couldn't believe my ears. All my life I had wanted to go to Italy. Now, to be invited to go, to be able to see Michelangelo's paintings on the ceiling of the Sistine Chapel in the Vatican was a dream come true.

As delighted as I was at this wonderful opportunity, I was reluctant to make such a trip by myself at seventy-five years old. Alan suggested that I might like to invite a fellow artist to join me. I immediately thought of my good friend, Joida Evans, who had lost her home, studio and art work in Katrina. When I contacted her, she was elated. Thus began one of the highlights of my life.

CHAPTER 53

"A DREAM COME TRUE"

Since my high school days when I studied world history, I had always wanted to see the work of the Old Masters and especially the paintings of Michelangelo on the ceiling of the Sistine Chapel in the Vatican. To combine this with an art workshop in the picturesque area of Tuscany was too good to be true!

There was much to be done before the trip; shopping for clothes, art supplies, new luggage. My friend, Joida , In Monroe, Louisiana was just as excited. The two week trip would be divided between time in Rome, Tuscany and Florence. Joida decided to extend her trip by visiting relatives in the country of Slovenia, which meant I would be returning from Italy by myself. I wasn't keen about flying back alone but figured I could make it since by then I would be a seasoned traveler.

We would start off with four days in Rome. The Sistine Chapel was our number one priority and we spent our first day there. There I stood in the famous chapel, craning my neck to take in all the unbelievable beauty of Michelangelo's famous painting. We had been instructed to not speak a word. The silence was golden. We were, indeed, on Holy Ground. My heart was overflowing with reverence and praise to God for this incredible gift to me.

We took in the usual tourist attractions, the lovely fountains and restaurants. We saved the Coliseum for our last night in Rome as we wanted to see it flooded by the red lights. But something happened on the way there that marred the trip for me. On the subway, a woman slammed herself against me and stole my camera with all the pictures I had made up to that point- including those at the Vatican, the famous sculpture of the Pieta, and many famous landmarks. I was sick to my soul. Others had made photos and were willing to share of course, but nothing could replace the "moment" for me when I had clicked the camera documenting my memories. I reported the loss to the police but was told that I would have to go across the city to file the claim and it was already quite late at night.. Our plane to Tuscany was leaving early the next morning. I had to accept my loss and move on.

Tuscany was everything I had been told to expect and even more beautiful than the pictures I had seen: the lovely villas with their red tile roofs, the vineyards bursting with luscious grapes, the olive groves, the fields being harvested. It was early October and the weather was perfect. Our villa was on a high hill overlooking the famous Serpentine Road which was a delight to see but not to travel. Our instructor, Alan Flattman, sketched some lovely demonstrations and inspired us all. The food in Tuscany was exceptionally good and the wine flowed abundantly. Evening meals lasted until 10:00 or 11:00 o'clock, therefore the nights were short.

In Florence we were on our own, so we did no painting, only sight-seeing. Florence is rich in architectural beauty. Joida had been there before and advised me of things I should be sure to see. At times we split up in our sight-seeing. I waited in line for over three hours to attend the Uffizi Art Gallery while she went elsewhere. Once inside the museum I had to climb six flights of stairs to see all the exhibits. I was more than exhausted and actually fell asleep at the dinner table that night!

Seeing all the beautiful artwork was worth the weariness, however. I felt rejuvenated by the many beautiful marble statues that were everywhere, including some Living Statues. It is popular in Italy for street actors, disguised as statues, to strike a pose for a long periods of time in locations where tourists pass by. They are rewarded when people drop coins in a container usually positioned by their feet. I got the surprise of my life when after watching a Statue stand still for a very long time, I went forward to drop some coins in his small bucket. As I did, he reached down and gave me a big hug. Joida caught the moment with her camera.

When I arrived back in the United States I was so tired I had to sit on my luggage for a while before I could catch the final leg of my flight from Atlanta. My 75 years had caught up with me but I'm glad I went. It was an unforgettable, inspirational, fun, and utterly exhausting experience!

CHAPTER 54

"MERRYWOOD MOVES ON"

Back at my home in Fairhope, my new life awaited me. It was time I got acquainted with my new "hometown" whose sheer beauty was invigorating after Katrina's awful destruction in Pass Christian.

Famous for its flowers, downtown Fairhope boasts floral beds that are never allowed to wilt or die. The beds are maintained during night so traffic is not disrupted. Each season brings with it new beauty. Everywhere I looked I saw something begging to be painted.

Though I was enjoying Fairhope, I still missed my former life, my many friends, my church, Pass Christian as it used to be, and of course my old home. I made frequent trips to Pass Christian to visit my daughter Dawn and my friends. Each time I passed Merrywood, I fought back tears. The old house sat neglected surrounded by a chain link barricade. What was to become of my old home?

I received a welcome call from Walmart one day. Merrywood was to be moved to a new location on Scenic Drive in downtown Pass Christian, just two doors down from the brand new Historical Society building. How wonderful! Such a prestigious location! For both its architectural and historical significance, it deserved to be there

Even though Walmart had donated the house to the city, the city had not been able to afford to have it moved. Along came Mike Gillespie of Cutting Edge Design. Mike had bought the property on Scenic Drive and wanted to restore a historic house. When he had seen the good "bones" of Merrywood, learned its sturdiness through numerous hurricanes, and discovered the fine materials that had gone into its construction, he was anxious to acquire it.

A deal was struck between Mike and city officials. Mike would have the house moved at his own expense, restore it and allow the city to use a portion of it for civic activities.

I couldn't wait to meet the man who so intrigued with my old home and its history. We made arrangements to meet at the Scenic Drive property. Mike impressed me with his congenial manner and I was delighted to discover he was a Christian. I knew Merrywood would be preserved and revered as it deserved.

Unable to attend the "moving day" event, I kept abreast of the proceedings via phone. A large contingent of my friends along with my daughter Dawn lined the beach highway, praying for a safe journey.

The big two-story house travelling down the highway appeared to be moving of its own volition, due to a controlled motor system installed under each of the house's four corners. Mike Gillespie waved through the windows as the old house crept down the highway. As it approached its new destination, he called me for special prayers. A highway median remained to be crossed and then the steep uphill embankment to Scenic Drive. I assured him that prayer warriors all along the way were also moving along with the house. Cheers rose when Merrywood was safely planted on its new turf.

The restoration of Merrywood was a major undertaking. Mike is a perfectionist and painstakingly restored the old house. He issued a standing invitation for me to visit there. I have been able to touch up a mural that I had painted many years ago. I also painted a portrait of Mr. Edward Price Bell, the original owner of Merrywood, which now hangs in the foyer. Mike tells me that a number of people have stopped by to see the house. Many have told him that they once attended prayer meetings or lived there for short periods. Today Merrywood still stands a well-loved bastion holding memories for many.

"No eye has seen, no ear has heard, no mind has conceived what God has prepared for those who love him." I Corinthians 2:9

Merrywood on the move...

Chapter 55
"Thy rod and Thy staff, they comfort me..."

I often questioned why I moved to Fairhope. It is a great place to live. I am nearer to my son and his family and I felt I could pursue my art interests there. I was in pretty good physical condition for a seventy-five year old. The fact that Nadine and I walked in the park almost daily contributed to that.

When Nadine and I walked in the park, I enjoyed the people I saw there- happy families, children playing, people walking their dogs, lovers strolling hand in hand, and yes, older couples arm in arm moving a little slower or enjoying the park benches. Companionship. That's what I missed. I missed my husband. I missed being married and having someone care about me, someone I needed to be accountable to, and I also realized I wanted someone to love, to grow older with, to fill the loneliness.

There were times when I wondered if I would ever marry again. There was certainly no one in my immediate future that I could see. How could I ever replace Jim in my heart? I knew that I had a lot to give to the right person but God would have to show me in no uncertain terms if something like that was meant to be. Perhaps I might meet someone who had also been a care-giver, who would understand where I was coming from, I mused. Or perhaps I might meet someone who was handicapped in some way and I could once again assume my role as caregiver. But did I really want that?

Why would I want to give up my new found freedom? I had never lived alone before and rather enjoyed the power to come and go as I pleased. Shop whenever I wanted. Eat out. Sleep late. Paint at all hours. Play the piano in the middle of the night. I had friends and family. Indeed, I was blessed! I determined in my heart to live each day to the fullest and enjoy my life. I was in God's hands.

I still greatly missed my church in Mississippi and had been actively seeking a new church and church family. I had heard good things about the Church on the Eastern Shore and decided to visit. It was a fairly new facility not far from my house. I didn't know what time the services were and when I arrived I found I was too late for the early service and too early for the late service. I waited in the lobby and enjoyed a cup of coffee as I looked over the church bulletin.

One of the greeters, a friendly and attractive woman, struck up a conversation with me. Her name was Pat Morgan and she asked if I was new in the area. In our exchange of conversation, we discovered we were both widows and had other things in common. Pat caught me off guard when she asked point blank, "Do you ever date?"

What a question and from a total stranger! I was taken aback but because she was so nice I didn't want to offend her and answered her question. "Well no, I have been a widow for five years but I have not dated anyone."

She then asked if I would consider going out to dinner with a nice man.....another blunt question! She went on to explain that her neighbor had lost his wife three years before and was lonely. According to her he was about my age and was a real southern gentleman. She assured me she would not suggest such a thing if he wasn't a very nice person.

Pat went on to say that this gentleman was a retired electrical engineer and regularly attended First Baptist Church in Fairhope. She, herself attended there on Sunday nights where she was involved in a Grief Share group. Her husband, a Baptist minister, had recently passed away. That's why she understood her neighbor's loneliness.

Then came the clincher. This nice gentleman was recovering from back surgery and was in a wheelchair. He could walk with a cane, she said, and was quite independent. He had been a care-taker to his wife before she died of cancer. Yes, he needed a cane to assist him with balance when he walked, but he had lived by himself for a number of years, doing his own cooking, laundry, shopping, housekeeping. Here it was! What had I said to God about who I might meet? A care-taker? A handicapped person?

I would not commit to dinner. I've got to think this over, I thought to myself. And I needed to get to know Pat better, so I invited her over to lunch one day. We found we were indeed kindred spirits. Once again she brought up the subject of going out to dinner with the widower. I was half-hearted when I committed to a blind dinner date, with Pat as chaperone.

When they arrived to pick me up Bill Sides was standing outside the car holding the door open for me. At first sight, the words from the familiar song "The First Time Ever I Saw Your Face", came into my mind. Strange. I had no idea what he looked like but he was quite handsome. For some reason I felt like I already knew him. Strange indeed!

Bill was an excellent conversationalist at dinner. In our exchange of getting to know one another, I found that he had three children, a son and two daughters. I had a son and two daughters. He had nine grandchildren, I had six. His son was a doctor, a medical missionary in China. Impressive.

I had issued an invitation that we have dessert back at my house. I showed him my small one room art studio and some of my paintings. I found out that he was a photographer as well as a musician. He played the French horn in the local Baldwin Pops Band. It was an amiable evening and I relaxed after meeting him. Pat just sat there smiling.

Pat called the next day to see what I thought about our meeting. I felt I should acknowledge my appreciation for the nice meal out, and asked for Bill's phone number. I waited a few days to call and when I did, he asked if I would like to go to lunch one day. I enjoyed his company and he seemed to enjoy mine. We began seeing each other more often, went to church together, had picnics and dinner out. It was nice to be courted by a well-mannered southern gentleman who made me feel very special.

Was I falling in love? Was this what love was really like at my age, or was it the companionship I enjoyed? Was this God? Was this the real reason I had moved to Fairhope?

Did I want to commit to a serious relationship at my age? Bill was two years older than me and he never once intimated that he was expecting any type of commitment from me. In time we met each other's families and immediately felt welcomed and at ease.

I had already visited First Baptist Church of Fairhope before I met Bill, but it was nice to know it was his home church. Of all the churches I had visited, I felt most comfortable there. It had recently recovered from a sanctuary fire and everyone was excited about being back in their beautiful facility. It was indeed a joy to be in this spacious auditorium with its great architectural design and huge stained glass window. I was especially impressed with the music, the large choir and excellent musicians. I had filled out a visitor's form soon after I attended the church, and was delighted when three very nice elderly ladies paid me a visit. They represented the JOY Sunday School class and encouraged me to visit their class. I did attend and enjoyed it very much. Betty Hansen, the teacher was excellent and well prepared. I joined the class and began to feel I was part of the church family.

I made an appointment to meet with Dr. Jerry Henry, the senior pastor. He was most gracious and welcomed me as a potential new member. In time I was asked to substitute teach the JOY class, which I considered to be a great honor. Later, I would be asked to teach a group of adults when they were studying the book of Revelation and was able to use my series of artistic color illustrations during my instruction. It was a joy to use my art once again for the Lord's work.

I always enjoyed Dr. Henry's sermons. It seemed that he made a special effort to preach often from the second chapter of Genesis where God says "It is not good for man to be alone". Was he looking directly at me?

Bill and I were becoming more and more attached to one another and spent many hours on the phone. One night over dessert, we approached the subject that we had both been wondering about. Where was our relationship headed? We were not exactly children and approached the subject of marriage from a logical standpoint. We expressed our love for each other which was rather obvious. But there were other things to consider, like where would we live. We both had homes of our own. Financially, we were both secure. We loved and accepted each other's families. Most of all, we were one in our faith in the Lord Jesus Christ.

As I pondered those words in Genesis where it says "It is not good for man to be alone", I knew that Bill really needed a wife. While he was very independent, it was at cost to his physical condition to have to do everything for himself. I could make his life easier in so many ways. But more importantly, like me, Bill needed companionship. When we counseled with Dr. Henry about getting married, he asked me the question, 'What do you want out of the marriage?

My answer was simple; "I want what every woman wants. I want to be loved."

How true that is. Woman's most basic need is to be loved for herself alone. While men also want to be loved, they also need to be respected. It was easy to respect Bill Sides. He is a man of exceptional integrity. He is kind, gentle, thoughtful, compatible, talented, as well as intelligent and wise. He does not compromise his principles but doesn't try to force his will on anyone else. He is a blessing from God.

We had a small but beautiful wedding with just immediate families and a few close friends present. On May 15, 2010 we exchanged rings, said our vows and headed for Destin, Florida where we spent our short honeymoon at a bed-n-breakfast on the beach with emerald waters tossing their waves across the sand..

"Delight yourself in the Lord and He will give you the desires of your heart." Psalm 37:4

CHAPTER 56

"A LEGACY"

In moments of reflection I wonder what kind of legacy I am leaving behind. I once told my children that if I had not left them the legacy of a Christian heritage, I would have failed them. I have tried to instill in them a deep faith in the Lord Jesus Christ. I have attempted to set a good example in godly living although I know I have often failed miserably. I am proud of my children and grandchildren, and now my seven great-grandchildren. It is my greatest desire that they live their lives in accordance with God's will. I pray that they will carry on the legacy that was left to them by their earthly father and mentor- Dr. James Carlos Tanner, who though confined to a wheelchair for most of his life, walked humbly before the Lord. A man who never felt God was punishing him, but rather keeping him from going astray.

Jim often quoted from Psalm 119:71, "It was good for me to be afflicted, so that I might learn your decrees." God is concerned with our hearts. In Psalms 147:10-11, we read, "His pleasure is not in the strength of the horse, nor is his delight in the legs of a man; the Lord delights in those who fear Him, who put their fear in his unfailing love."

The Bible teaches us that "God has set eternity in our hearts." (Ecclesiastes 3:11) Who among us has not thought about eternity? Where will we spend it? What will it be like? Our utmost concern should be to live our lives so that we might spend eternity with the one who created us in His image, God Almighty, maker of all that is seen and unseen. Jesus Christ has made that possible.

I like to think that even a house can leave a legacy. It is my prayer that Merrywood, dedicated to God so many years ago, will cause people who enter it to feel the Holy Spirit lingering there. God did not spare it from many hurricanes for no reason.

It was recently my great pleasure to attend a wonderful event at the beautifully restored Merrywood. My long-time friends, Jim and Jane Kramer celebrated their 60th wedding anniversary there. They especially wanted to have their celebration there since they had their 50th wedding anniversary at Merrywood after Katrina had ravaged their own home. It was a lovely occasion and many in attendance were delighted to once again be in the old house which holds such wonderful memories.

What will become of Merrywood?

The year is 2016 as I draw this book to a close. At present, Merrywood is leased to three ministers who are involved in a private enterprise of building homes in a neighboring town. They are enthusiastic about living in the house where so many prayer meetings took place and which was the birthplace of the Church of the Good Shepherd.

I no longer fret over Merrywood's future because of all that God has already done. I believe that its loving restoration has not been in vain. It is my heart's desire that the house always be used for God's glory. May the legacy of Merrywood continue.

Is it possible that this book could leave a legacy? According to Dr. Mark and Mary Ann Wyatt of Wyatt House Publishing, "A book is a legacy that can outlive us all." It is my prayer that you have been drawn closer to Jesus as you have read "To Walk a Country Mile".

I close this book with lines from one of my favorite poems by Rudyard Kipling:

L'Envoi

When earth's last picture is painted, and the tubes are twisted and dried,
When the oldest colors have faded, and the youngest critic has died,
We shall rest, and faith, we shall need it –lie down for aeon or two,
Till the Master of All Good workmen shall set us to work anew.

PART II
GOD STORIES

"I'd Rather Be in Jail . . ."

I tore open the envelope, always happy to receive a letter from my friend Nancy in Memphis. Her opening words stunned me, "I'd rather be in jail than any place I know." What was she thinking? Who in their right mind would rather be in jail?

I read on. Nancy had become involved with a Christian jail ministry at a large jail in the city of Memphis, Tennessee. She was elated at the fruit the ministry was bearing among the female inmates. "I can't wait for you to come to Memphis and go with me to the jail," she wrote. Her words shook me. Me? in jail ministry? No way.

I was already serving the Lord . . . in my own way . . . working in my local church, hosting weekly Bible studies in my home, visiting the sick in the hospital, preparing food where there was a need, opening my home for traveling evangelists. What more could one person do?

Her words haunted me, "I can't wait for you to go to jail with me." Well, I could wait, forever I thought. I'd never visited a jail, never knew anyone personally who was in jail. That type of ministry was fine for others, but not for me.

A few weeks later I found myself in Memphis visiting our daughter and her family. I hesitated to call Nancy because I didn't want to disappoint her by not going to the jail with her. "Oh, I'm so excited you are here!" she exclaimed on the phone, "I'll pick you up tomorrow at one o'clock."

I didn't sleep a wink that night. I'll call her first thing tomorrow and tell her I can't make it. I couldn't make the call. I was a nervous wreck. I prayed fervently, "Oh, Lord, I've tried to do all you've asked me to do before. Why am I having such a hard time with this? If you are really in this, then please give me something from your Word to encourage me." I picked up my Bible and let it fall open where it might, since I didn't know where to start looking. As God is my witness, my eyes fell on these words, "Remember those in prison as if you were their fellow prisoner . . ." Hebrews 13:3 (NIV)

How plain could it get? Clearly God had spoken. On the drive to the jail, Nancy told me that the hardest part was hearing the steel doors clang behind you as you were shut in with the prisoners. Help. Lord, what am I to say? Watching Nancy move among the captive audience and the joyous response of their hugs, I began to understand why she had said what she did, "I'd rather be in jail than any place I know."

God took away my anxiety and replaced it with compassion and love for these hurting souls who were hanging on every word of my testimony. And what was my testimony? No, I had not sinned as some in their cells had, but "all have sinned and fallen short of the glory of God." Romans 3:23 And I took them on a walk down the Roman Road. "But God demonstrated his love for us in this: " While we were still sinners in Christ died for us." Romans 5:8. And "For the wages of sin is death, but the gift of God is eternal life in Christ Jesus our Lord." Romans 6:23 Again, "If you confess with your mouth. Jesus is Lord and believe in your heart that God raised Him from the dead, you will be saved. For it is with your mouth that you confess and are saved." Romans 10:9-10 "For everyone who calls on the name of the Lord will be saved." Romans 10:13

"Remember those in prison as if you were their fellow prisoners."

"Mustard Seed Faith"

I stood back from the full-length mirror and admired the fit of the dress, perfect in every way. "The Lord sure has good taste in clothes," I thought to myself as I recounted the events of the day. The main thing on my agenda for that day was a trip to the mall to shop for a new dress. My husband Jim, and I were planning a fall vacation and I was in need of a basic black dinner dress.

But, first things first. I always liked to have my devotional time early in the morning, before the day got too busy and crowded out my quiet time with the Lord. I opened my Bible and began to read in the fourth chapter of the book of Mark about the mustard seed. "Concerning the kingdom of God", Mark writes in verses 31-32, "It is like a mustard seed, which is the smallest of all the seeds on the earth; yet when it is sown it grows up and becomes the greatest of all shrubs and puts forth large branches, so that the birds of the air can make nests in its shade."

"How big is your mustard tree?" The thought came to me as if the Lord had spoken. "Huh?" I questioned, "What do you mean, how big is my mustard tree?" Puzzled, I was reflecting on the matter when another thought popped into my mind, "You need to tell Joyce that her mustard seed has grown large and many people have made nests in the branches of her faith." Where did this come from? What is going on? Am I hearing things or imagining them? Joyce? Oh, okay Lord, Joyce. My dear friend, Joyce Watts, had been diagnosed with cancer and despite all medical treatments and the prayers of literally hundreds of people, she seemed to be losing the battle. She was a very strong Christian, a Bible teacher and leader among women. People revered her and her husband Frank, and sought them out as prayer warriors and counselors. She was indeed, a woman of great faith, and yet while she believed for others to be healed, she found her faith wavering when it came to her own healing. She was discouraged and time was running out.

Perhaps God wanted her to know that her own faith was like the tiny mustard seed, and many had found nests in her mustard tree. I know that I had, and she needed to know how important her example had been in my life.

I looked at my watch, 9:20. It was Wednesday morning; where would Joyce be? At Mary Emerson's house, of course. Each Wednesday, Joyce led a ladies Bible study at her friend's house. It would begin at 9:30. There was no time to lose.

Am I hearing from you, Lord? I knew the answer. Nevertheless, I prayed all the way down the highway the ten miles to Mary's house. When I arrived, cars were everywhere and I could hardly find a parking place. I tried to slip in quietly since I was running late. Mary greeted me warmly as I told her, "The Lord told me to come." The room was crowded, all chairs were taken, but there was an empty place on the floor, right next to Joyce.

She was not the speaker that morning. There was a special guest, Sara Gibson, of Meridian was teaching on "The Anointing". It was powerful and I made lots of notes. "I know why I came," I thought, "I really needed to hear this." But, there I was, sitting next to Joyce with a message from the Lord for her. As the meeting wound down, I shared with Joyce what I felt God wanted her to know: her mustard seed had grown into a tall bush and many people had made nests in the branches of her faith. Her eyes filled with tears as she gratefully acknowledged her need to hear those words.

A wonderful time of fellowship followed, and I almost forgot my need to go shopping. I would have to hurry- the day was slipping by. I went to my favorite stores in the mall but began to feel discouraged when I couldn't find what I needed. I was about to learn a valuable lesson in prayer. "Lord," I prayed, "I delivered the message to Joyce. Could you please help me find the right dress?"

A few more shops and still nothing. I was about to leave the mall as I passed the nicest, most expensive store of all. "I really can't afford to look in here," I thought. Nevertheless, I found myself heading for the petite dress section. "Another waste of time," I thought as I started to exit the store. Then I saw it! A single black dress, alone on a round dress rack. It was in the junior dress department. I would never have thought to look there, but it seemed to be waiting for me. I looked at the size, 8, perfect. I looked at the price, $50, unbelievable for this store, and I really liked the style. I headed for the dressing room.

I knew it was mine- perfect fit, good style, nice fabric; yes, this would be ideal. I began to thank the Lord for leading me to the right dress, for answering my prayer. As I began to put the dress back on its hanger, my eyes riveted on the label in the back of the neck. I couldn't believe it! I was seeing things! I was completely overcome! There, in embroidered letters were two words, Mustard Seed! My hands trembled, I wanted to cry, I wanted to shout! Who would believe it! Nothing else on the label except Mustard Seed.

I felt no need to try to tell the whole story to the clerk. She probably wouldn't have believed or understood the significance. But Jim would, and my friends would. I couldn't wait to share it and practically floated home.

The next day was a very busy day and I never made the intended call to Joyce to share about the dress. However, it was Thursday and the night for our weekly Prayer meeting in our home. Who should walk in but Joyce and Mary. I was able to share my incredible story with everyone.

They all agreed, I have a Designer's Original!

"The Merrywood Sign"

The doorbell rang as Jim and I were enjoying a quiet Sunday afternoon sitting by a cozy fire, playing dominoes.

I opened the door to see two teenage girls standing on the front porch. One of them had her hands behind her back as she spoke, Mrs. Tanner, my name is Jenny (not her real name), and well, I stole your Merrywood sign." With that she brought forth the wooden sign from behind her back. My mouth fell open in surprise!

I had been upset when I discovered the sign was missing. I had made it myself, cutting the wood design with a jig-saw, painted it white, hand-painted a magnolia flower on it and the name of our house: Merrywood, Built in 1927. It had hung out front by our street for two years or more. I knew it had been stolen because the chains on which it was attached were still on the post.

I felt both angry and violated. Why would anyone want to steal my sign? It wouldn't mean anything to anyone else. I did the only thing I knew to do, I turned to prayer. I asked God to take away my anger and to deal with whoever stole the sign., to work on their conscious and cause them to return it to me.

Over a year had passed since that prayer and now my sign had come home! Jenny placed the sign in my hands and continued, "I stole the sign, but I got saved and God showed me I needed to return the sign and ask for forgiveness."

It took a lot of courage for this young lady to come forward like this. I opened my arms to her and told her I forgave her. What a remarkable answer to prayer! God answered my prayer exactly as I had asked, moving on the heart of the one who stole the sign to return it. God always answers prayers, whether immediately, delayed or in ways we don't always understand.

We invited the young girls to join us on Thursday nights for our prayer group and Bible studies, which they did. Their story is a real testimony to the power of prayer.

"Chance Encounter"

After enjoying a scenic drive on the beautiful Blue Ridge Parkway for several hours, my husband and I decided we needed to exit the slow moving traffic. "Perhaps we had better get off at the next exit," Jim said. Soon the sign for Buena Vista came into view. As we pulled off the parkway we noticed an ice cream stand nearby. It would be nice to have a refreshing cone after the hot day.

We pulled into a parking space next to a car that also had a Mississippi car tag like we did. I noticed that it was a Washington County tag also. Our daughter, Debby and her husband, Lewis Levy lived in Greenville, Mississippi, which is in Washington County. The car also had a Christian bumper sticker.

A middle-aged couple stood in line ahead of me, waiting their turn to order. We greeted each other remarking how good the ice cream was going to taste after the warm day. "I see you have a Washington County, Mississippi tag. My daughter lives in Greenville," I said. I was pleased to know that they too, lived in Greenville. I shared Debby's and Lewis' names, but they had not met them.

As we shared in more conversation we discovered that they knew some mutual friends who were active in Methodist Renewal Missions. As we enjoyed our ice cream, we realized that we had something else in common.

We were returning from visiting the 700 Club in Virginia Beach, and they were on their way to visit the 700 Club.

As we stood around the car chatting, Frank Forseman asked if Debby and Lewis had found a church home in Greenville. I knew that they had visited a number of churches but had not settled on one. She was Methodist, he was Catholic. Frank asked if it was okay to get their address and phone number so he could invite them to a young adult Sunday school class he was organizing in his Methodist Church.

I wrote the information on a slip of paper and handed it to Frank. When he saw the name of the street, Mary Street, he exclaimed, "I can't believe it! We live right around the corner! I pass their house every morning when I walk the dog." A coincidence? No indeed, God was up to something. We parted as new friends and headed west as they headed east.

Two weeks passed and we had an exciting phone call from Debby. "Mother, the most unusual thing happened today. The doorbell rang and a man named Frank Forseman stood there and told me he had met you and Dad at an ice cream stand in Buena Vista, Virginia. He invited us to visit a Sunday school class that he teaches." She was more than a little excited and here is why.

She and Lewis had been deliberating about where to go to church, and the very night before Frank's visit, she had prayed a significant prayer; "Oh, God, I don't know where we are supposed to go to church. Please send someone to our door to invite us to visit their church and I will take that as a sign from You." She had a quick answer to her prayer, although God had set it in motion two weeks before during our chance encounter at the ice cream stand. ("Before they call, I will answer; while they are still speaking, I will hear." Isaiah 65:24)

The story didn't end there. Debby and Lewis attended Frank's Sunday school class and found their church home. They were very happy, active and made lots of friends their age. Frank tucked Lewis under his wing and mentored him in his Christian walk. Frank was there when their first child was born, sharing in the anxiety and the joy. He was always there for them.

When Frank was diagnosed with cancer, they were devastated. They prayed and prayed for his healing. His was a hard death and for a while

Lewis was angry at God for taking Frank away. I reminded him that Frank had taught him how to live, and showed him how to die. He was safe and well in his eternal home.

Many years have passed and many changes have taken place, but the godly influence of Frank Forseman is everlasting.

"For I know the plans I have for you, declares the Lord, "plans to prosper you and not to harm you, plans to give you hope and a future." Jeremiah 29:11

"THE RIGHT MOTEL"

I was upset with Jim as we approached Knoxville, Tennessee on Interstate 40. I had been looking forward to attending the World's Fair that was in progress there at the time. After all, I had not been able to attend the one in New Orleans even though we lived only sixty miles away.

Jim was exhibiting a negative attitude toward the whole idea, even though we had driven 600 miles to get there. Actually, this was to be the first stop on our vacation to the east coast. "Just drop me off at a hotel," he said, "And you can go see your precious World's Fair." Those curt words poured cold water on my plans, and I might add, my spirit.

I could understand where he was coming from- he was tired- he hated being in crowds with his wheelchair, there never being a clear path. As for me, I'd probably never have another chance to attend a World's Fair.

I'd been watching for motel signs as we neared Knoxville. The sun was beginning to set as I chose an exit that advertised a lot of motel signs. 'No Vacancy' signs were everywhere. Finding a room of any kind was going to be hard, and especially a handicapped room. At length, we found a motel with rooms available, but while I was waiting in line to register, a tour bus arrived with a large group of loud, excited people intent on having a good time. Obviously, they had reservations.

I began to feel in my spirit what Jim had been feeling all along. We

258

didn't belong here, not at this motel, not at the World's Fair. I returned to the car and said, "O.K., you win," I said, "You wouldn't enjoy the party atmosphere, and neither would I." We got back on the interstate and headed east.

We rode in silence for miles and finally Jim spoke, "I'd really like to find a place miles away from the Fair crowds." After a while we spotted a Ramada Inn sign still fifty miles away. We were already tired, now we were getting hungry and ready to find a resting place. The Ramada Inn kept getting closer- Morristown Exit, the sign read. "I had a patient at the Memphis VA Hospital who was from Morristown," Jim spoke up, "I wonder if he's still here."

Finally, the awaited exit came into view and to my delight the Ramada Inn sat high on a hill overlooking the rolling countryside. To our relief, they had a handicapped accessible room available. As I unloaded the car, Jim explored the facilities. This would do fine- easy access to the dining room and to our delight they were still serving supper.

Several things about the atmosphere of the place impressed me. I noticed Christian tracts had been placed in our room, as well as in the lobby. The staff was most accommodating and after a satisfying meal we went into the comfortable lobby to look around. My eye was drawn to a lady sitting on a sofa. She seemed to be in distress and was crying. My heart went out to her and I sat down beside her to inquire if I could help her. She related that a relative had been in an accident and the situation was critical. She was waiting for someone to come for her. I asked if I could pray for her and while she was surprised at my offer, she allowed me to do so.

Back in our room, I told Jim I felt like whoever owned the motel must be Christian because the tell-tale signs were everywhere- the Bible opened to a particular portion of scripture- the peaceful atmosphere, the tracts. We had a wonderful night's sleep and I was actually reconciled about missing the World's Fair. Finding this nice place and being able to minister to the lady in the lobby made me feel we were in God's will.

The best was yet to come. When we went into the dining room for breakfast, we were warmly greeted by our hostess. "I'm familiar with wheelchairs," she said, "One of the owners of this place is in one." "I had a patient from Morristown on my ward at the VA Hospital in Memphis," Jim spoke up, "His name was Randy Kington. Would you happen to know him?"

The hostess broke into a big smile, "Why, yes! He's the one! He's a co-owner of this motel. In fact, he'll probably be here for his usual breakfast." Just to make sure, she put in a call to him.

Wow! Now we really felt like we were indeed in the right place. Nothing pleased us more than feeling we were being orchestrated by the Lord. Shortly afterward, a handsome young man in a wheelchair came rolling up to our table. "Dr. Tanner!" he exclaimed, "I can't believe it's really you!" He seemed overjoyed to see Jim. After introductions, he joined us for breakfast, and began sharing his life after leaving the VA Hospital. While serving in the military, he had been seriously injured leaving him as a paraplegic.

Randy told us, "When I was a patient at the VA Hospital in Memphis, and experiencing depression over my condition, I would hear you coming down the hall, Dr. Tanner, whistling and greeting everybody and I said to my room-mate, 'What's with this guy? He's in a wheelchair, too. How can he be so happy?'

"Oh, don't you know? He's a Christian and has a wonderful attitude'" The roommate replied. Randy went on, "I watched you over the months, as you were my doctor. I got to thinking, 'If he can make it in this life with that kind of attitude, then so can I.' And so you see, Dr. Tanner, you changed my life."

Randy went on to share with us how he returned to Morristown after his hospital stay, accepted his physical limitations, studied to become a certified public accountant and a business man. He had married a good wife and they had adopted two Asian children. He had become a productive member of society, but most importantly, he had become a Christian.

What an incredible story, what a thrill and joy to see what God had done in Randy's life. He bought our breakfast, and assured us there would always be a room available to us, there or in his home.

We needed to move on, but when I think what we might have missed if we had spent the night in Knoxville, I was so glad we made the right decision. We might never have known the blessing of the Randy Kington story.

How it encouraged Jim to know he had a part in the life changing experience. Nothing at the World's Fair could have given us this much pleasure.

Truly a God story!!!!!!!

"A Rainbow for Kevin"

The late September storm was relentless. All day the rain, thunder and lightning had raged. I paced the floor of our son's home in rural Cantonment, Florida, waiting for a break in the weather. My husband and I were anxious to get to the hospital in nearby Pensacola. I glanced at my watch—four o'clock. It had been exactly six days since Kevin's accident.

On September 22, 1999, two months after his fourteenth birthday, our grandson Kevin was involved in a terrible automobile accident while riding home from school with a friend. Kevin was thrown from the pickup truck which flipped over several times, landing upright on top of him and trapping him under the rear axle, His rescue was nothing short of a miracle and is a whole story in itself. Now he lay in Sacred Heart Hospital in Pensacola, with a severe head injury and other less serious injuries. He was in a coma from the beginning.

My husband, Jim, a retired medical doctor, and I had immediately driven over from our home in Mississippi to be with our son and his family and to help out however we might be needed. We were all exhausted from lack of sleep and stress over Kevin's critical condition.

As long time Christians, we had begun praying for Kevin the moment we got the awful news. Prayer vigils were taking place all around the country on behalf of our grandson. Our son, his wife , and their other two children were committed Christians. Their church, pastors and many friends had immediately rallied to their support.

Still, anxiety weighed heavily on our hearts. We used the slacking of the rain as an opportunity to get into our van and head for the hospital. "Oh, dear God, please give us some sort of sign that Kevin is going to be alright," I prayed. Thick dark clouds still hovered low around us as we pulled onto the highway. A half mile down the road as we were rounding a curve on a high ridge of the rural countryside, I gasped at the unfolding scene. As though on cue from some unseen director, the dark rolling clouds were drawn back on each side as curtains on a theatre stage. What happened next took my breath away! There in a patch of clear sky was a perfect and highly ached rainbow!

"Look, Jim, oh look! A rainbow! It must be the sign that I asked for." Almost as quickly as it had appeared, the clouds covered it, as if the stage curtain had been closed. The whole scenario could not have lasted more than forty-five seconds. Forty-five seconds – a moment in time, but what a moment. If it had happened a fraction of a moment earlier or later, we would have missed it. My heart filled with joy and hope and thankfulness for God's provision of the rainbow. I began to thank Him as I prayed, "Dear Lord, you set a rainbow in the sky as a covenant with Noah that You would never again destroy the earth with a flood (Genesis 9:12-17). The Bible tells us that You remember Your covenant forever and the word You commanded for a thousand generations (Psalms 105:8). Thank You for this sign from heaven. We believe that You hear our prayers and will heal Kevin."

Even though we could see no visible change in Kevin's condition when we reached the hospital, we were all encouraged over the "sign". Later that evening, as I was having my devotional time, I was further comforted with these words in the daily devotional book I was reading: the message for that day, September 28, 1999 was entitled "A Sure Sign from Heaven."

The following day we again found ourselves waiting for the rain to stop so we could get in our van and head to the hospital. Kevin's condition was the same: still comatose, head swollen almost twice in size, blood pressure skyrocketing, and heart rate extremely irregular. The doctors had put a stint into his brain days before to try to relieve some of the pressure building inside his skull He had a broken shoulder, bruises, contusions, and his bodily functions were far from normal. Despite our wonderful sign of the rainbow, it was hard to keep our hopes up.

As we were driving I half-heartedly said, "God is setting the stage for another rainbow." In my heart I was silently praying, "Lord, I do believe yesterday's rainbow was a sign from you that Kevin is going to be all right. If you were to show us another rainbow it would remove all doubt and a third would be totally awesome."

Everything was essentially the same as the day before---same spot in the road, same hillside and curve---except the clouds were not quite as heavy. I found myself looking in the direction of yesterday's rainbow and to my utter amazement, there it was! This time there was no need for the clouds to part. The rainbow was not as highly arched as before. It stretched long and low, barely over the treetops. If I had not been looking for it, I might have easily missed it. But there it was in all its glory and the clouds did not cover it as we passed by.

How our hearts rejoiced. Two rainbows in two days! How often does anyone see such a thing? And especially in direct answer to prayer! We called ahead to the hospital to share the good news with Kenny and Tammy. Since the accident, they had hardly left Kevin's side and were utterly exhausted. This second sign was a tremendous encouragement to us all. Still, there seemed to be no change in Kevin's condition.

The following day my husband and I needed to return to Mississippi. The storms of the past two days has dissipated and the weather was clearing as we headed west on Interstate 10. A spectacular sunset was unfolding as we traveled along, becoming increasingly beautiful with each passing mile. The sky was a panorama of aquas, pinks, oranges, yellows, and purples with dramatic cloud formations and brilliance beyond compare. It seemed to encompass us, even from behind. I could not remember a more glorious sunset. Others must have felt the same way as cars were literally pulling off the interstate to enjoy heaven's show.

As an artist, the scene cried out to be painted. Then I remembered what I was doing the afternoon I received word of Kevin's accident. I was in my art studio painting a sunset. But no artist could capture the incredible beauty of the scene before me now.

"Well I certainly can't expect to see a rainbow today," I said to myself. "Whoever heard of a rainbow in a sunset?"

Two beautiful white clouds floated in the distance above the sunset in almost the shape of large white doves. Then came the most unusual phenomenon. There in the sky, slightly above and to the right of the sun was a huge shining ball. It was glowing white, silvery, and golden at the same time. We thought it was the moon at first but that was impossible. There was something coming out of the side of the ball. It was shaped like a sword and was painted all the colors of the rainbow.

A third rainbow! And it was breathtaking! I began to weep for joy. I was reminded of the scriptures where the word of God is referred to as a sword, (Ephesians 6:17, Hebrews 4:12). God was reminding me again that He honors His word and keeps His covenant.

The sunset's colors had faded by the time we reached home, but our spirits were uplifted. It was prearranged that we would have guests that evening. Kevin's former pastor and his wife Charlotte, now living in Texas, had been to visit him in the hospital. We invited them to stay the night as they were heading back to Texas.

As I greeted them at the door, the first words out of Charlotte's mouth were, "We saw the most beautiful rainbow except it wasn't shaped like a rainbow...it was long and straight...."

"Like a sword!?" I interrupted.

Together we rejoiced in God's continuing encouragement to us. But He was not finished yet. I was reading my daily devotional book the next day. This particular selection had been written about recovery from surgery and began, "It's over, you can wake up now...". And indeed, shortly thereafter, a nurse came into Kevin's hospital room and said the very same words: "You can wake up now."

Kevin did wake up out of his coma. While his recovery was not immediate, he was home from the hospital and rehab center in seven weeks and two days.

It was a long road but Kevin worked hard and recovered. He possesses a special kind of care and compassion for others. God still has big plans for Kevin Tanner. When your situation looks hopeless, look for your rainbow, remembering God's covenant to his people for a thousand generations.

Sunset on Interstate 10

Her Name is Frances"

I looked at my dining room table, covered with paperwork. It would take me days to complete the follow-up letters, the thank you notes, the bank deposits, etc. after the wonderful Holy Spirit Conference we had just experienced over the weekend. Jim was the co-chairman; I did the legwork. I didn't need an early morning phone call and I was hoping it wouldn't take long as I picked up the receiver. "Hello."

The voice on the line said, "My name is Frances Coggin. Can you pray with me to receive the baptism in the Holy Spirit?"

How direct could someone be? What a question, and why to me? I had prayed for people before on the subject, but always in a group or with someone who was much more experienced at leading people in this kind of prayer. But, never one on one. I felt inadequate but what could I say? "Can you come over?" I heard myself ask. I prayed a brief but fervent prayer, "HELP, LORD!"

Fifteen minutes later the doorbell rang and there she stood, holding a small baby in her arms, an attractive woman in her mid-thirties. I invited her in and offered a cup of coffee. "I'm curious as to how you came to call me." I said. She was quite serious as she related how she was sitting at the breakfast table that very morning, eating a bowl of cereal, when she saw the words "get up and go" on the cereal box. Believing she was hearing from the Lord, she said, "Get up and go where, Lord?"

Her story poured forth. She had been seeking to know more about the Holy Spirit and had gone to her Episcopal priest the week before and asked him to pray for her to re ceive the Holy Spirit. After some reflection her told her, "I'm sorry, I can't help you, but I do have some information on the subject." He reached down into the trash basket beside his office desk and pulled out a brochure advertising the conference to be held at the Methodist Seashore Assembly in Biloxi, Mississippi. The mention of the brochure had my attention. It had been my responsibility to distribute the brochures in the local area and I had taken the job seriously. I got the phone directory out and prayed about who to send the brochures to, with the information on the upcoming Holy Spirit. Conference. We had a wonderful line-up of speakers and this was an interdenominational event. Obviously, I had included this Episcopal priest in the mail-outs.

Frances had good intentions of attending the conference, but at the last minute, there was a family conflict. Earlier this morning, she had looked up the telephone number that was listed on the brochure to call for information about the conference.

The voice who answered her phone call was that of a retired Methodist pastor, now serving as the superintendent of the Assembly facilities. He had attended the conference, however, he did not embrace the new charismatic movement that was growing among Methodist churches in the area.

"Hmmmm, you say you want to receive the baptism is the Holy Spirit?" he said in response to her query, "Hmmmm, well ahem.....I'm sorry.....I can't help you." Frances was really disappointed. This was now the second minister of the gospel who could not, or would not, pray with her. "Where do you live?" he inquired of her. "Pass Christian." was her reply. "Oh, let me give you the name of a lady who might be able to help you."
That is how Frances came to call me. Now I'm thinking, this is God at work.

I was intrigued with her persistent desire to seek the Holy Spirit, but I knew nothing about her, whether she was a true believer, whether she attended church, or even if she understood what she really wanted. I asked her to share something of her background, and was relieved to know she had understood and received her salvation. She was just a hungry soul seeking a deeper walk and wanting to drink from the well of living water.

We talked for a long while and then it was time to pray. Her precious baby was an angel during this time, sleeping through it all. She laid the baby on the sofa and together we got on our knees to pray. As God began to work, we could sense the presence of the sweet Holy Spirit in the room with us. Softly, Frances began to laugh, and her joy could not be contained. She could not stop laughing. When she finally regained composure she said to me, "Oh, I forgot to tell you, I've been diagnosed as being depressed. The first thing the Holy Spirit did for her was set her free from that label.

Later, as Frances was leaving, she said, "I just remembered the name of the cereal I was eating this morning: *Total*! Now I'm the *Total* Woman." We shared a happy laugh as one of the most popular books of the day was entitled *The Total Woman*.

Today, many years later, I'm happy to say that Frances Coggin is one of the strongest, most enthusiastic Christians I know. She now lives in Israel where she metand married a Messianic Jewish believer. Together, they are serving Jesus and awaiting His return.

PART III
IT WAS THURSDAY NIGHT

"JOY"

"Do you know who I would really like to see?" my husband Jim asked me as he sat next to the fireplace waiting for people to arrive for our weekly Bible study, prayer meeting. "I would love to see Joy." He continued, "I miss her so much and I don't even know how to get in touch with her since she moved to Chicago."

Indeed, we did miss Joy. She was in the Air Force and had been stationed at a nearby Air Force base for a while. I don't know how she found out about our Thursday night home group, but she began attending regularly, and what a blessing she was. She was pretty as a picture, blonde, petite, and had the voice of an angel. Her guitar was her side-kick and she played it with a great anointing. She composed many of the songs she sang and played for us, always living up to her name of "Joy".

Jim's words were hardly out of his mouth when the doorbell rang. As I opened the door my mouth fell open in disbelief! There stood Joy with her side-kick guitar!

It Was Thursday Night!

"$1.37"

She was a new face in the crowd. It was a sad face, especially her eyes. She had nice features, but wore no makeup and her clothing spoke of hard times. Her name was Lynn. It was not unusual for strangers to show up at our home prayer group. I never knew how she found out about our meeting, but here she was, shy, quiet and sad. She said nothing that I recall, but listened intently to whoever the speaker was that night.

She left a little before the meeting was over and as I saw her to the front door, she stuck some money in my blouse pocket. "Take it," she said, "It's all I have." I looked at the money, a dollar bill and thirty-seven cents in change. "If this is all you have, then you should keep it for yourself," I said. "That little bit won't do me any good," she replied.

Following her outside, I found out she lived two blocks away in an apartment complex, but was about to be evicted because she couldn't pay the rent. Her husband was an alcoholic and they had two young children. They were out of food. She was right, the $1.37 wouldn't have done much good. She did the best thing; she planted a seed.

Later I shared with the remainder of the group inside and we prayed and decided on a course of action. A love offering was taken to buy food and I would approach our church about helping with the rent.

It Was Thursday Night!

"BROTHERLY LOVE"

We had to bring in extra chairs, people were sitting on the stairs, inside the bedroom with the French doors opened out; you might say the place was packed. There were a number of first time visitors that night; among them was Ron Hurlbert, well known in the area as the preaching policeman. He had made a name for himself, preaching and singing in churches and on radio. We were delighted to have him and some of his friends attend our home group. Admittedly, I was a little nervous and hoped everything went well.

It did, for a while. About halfway through the meeting the front door opened and a man came stumbling in, so drunk he could hardly stand. He reeked of whiskey. I was mortified! Nothing like this had ever happened to us before.

We knew him, of course, he had been a regular at our meetings for a while. He never had much to say, so we really didn't know for sure about his walk with the Lord.

He found himself a seat among some of the people at one end of the living room and settled down. I breathed a sigh of relief hoping he would behave himself because I surely didn't know what to do about him. Everything was fine, until he fell out of his chair. Needless to say, this was a great disruption to the Bible study. He started sobbing and apologizing, saying he had been at a local bar, the Fox's Den, and had started drinking. He remembered it was Thursday night and was ashamed about his back-sliding, and somehow, found his way to our house.

Some of the brothers helped him off the floor, and out onto the front porch swing. They prayed with him and tried to sober him up with hot coffee. It was a little difficult to get things back on track as far as the prayer group was concerned, but finally it was over. I apologized to the visiting policeman and his friends. "This kind of thing has never happened before." I said, "I do hope you will come back again." "I will," replied Ron, "The thing that impressed me the most was the way the brothers showed love to that man. They really cared about him and helped restore him. I'll come back." And he did.

It Was Thursday Night!

"I WANT TO TESTIFY"

One of the most important things about gathering together for Christian fellowship is hearing the testimonies of other people. It is faith building beyond words. During the years of our Thursday night prayer group, we regularly sang a little song, "I Want to Testify". The chorus went, "I want to testify, I want to tell, what the Lord has done for me…" We called them popcorn testimonies. People would pop up after the chorus and in a nutshell tell what the Lord had done for them recently. It was cause for great rejoicing, and giving praise to God.

The Bible says in Revelation 12:11 that "We overcome by the blood of the lamb and the word of our testimony". Sharing with others what God has done in our lives, answered prayers, testimonies of miracles, not only helps us overcome, but others who hear these things. A couple of stories stand out in my memory that were shared in our home meetings.

Hank's story #1: Hank Lero was one of the early leaders in our Thursday night group. We attended the same church, which had just held a missions conference in order to promote financial and prayer support for missionaries. Hank and his wife, Carolyn, were so moved by the needs of the missionaries, that they made a sizeable faith pledge at the Sunday morning service. A faith pledge meant that you expected God to provide the funds to meet your pledge over and above your ordinary expenses. When Hank

276

went to bed that Sunday night, he prayed a simple prayer, "Lord, I don't want to have to drag this pledge out, the missionaries need it. You know I don't have the money so I'm asking You to bring it on in quickly."

The very next day when Hank went to pick up his mail from the mailbox, he found his prayer was answered. There in his hand, was an unexpected check for the exact amount of his pledge. He immediately took the check down to the church and gave praise to Jehovah Jireh, our provider. What a testimony to the faithfulness of God and what an encouragement to the church to believe for their own faith pledges.

Hank's story #2: Hank worked for a government contractor at the nearby NASA space center. Once the project was completed, Hank found himself without a job. As the father of eight children, this indeed, was a major problem. He applied for all kinds of jobs, picked up a few odd jobs and prayed for full time employment. Weeks passed and still no permanent job. A devout believer, Hank was studying his Bible one day when he read the words, "A man reaps what he sows." (Galatians 6:7) Hank wondered if this verse could apply to his own situation. He decided to put it to the test. He began to "sow work". He helped a man roof his house at no charge. He sowed a day's work by helping another man bale hay, again at no salary. For several more days, Hank began to sow work wherever he saw a need and at no charge.

Then an offer came for a full time position. How he praised God, but lo, another offer came that was even better. God wasn't through yet. A third full time job offer came in rapid succession, which turned out to be the perfect one. God's principles always work and can be applied to all areas of our lives. Whatever your own need is, sow to that need, whether it is financial, spiritual, or job related, plant a seed. Need more love? Sow love. Put God to the test.

It Was Thursday Night!

"HOUSE OF PRAYER"

"Come in please." I ushered her into the living room and onto the sofa. She was on her way home from the doctor's office where she had received the dreaded report, breast cancer. She lived on our street, was married and the mother of a young daughter. She said she had attended our Thursday night prayer meeting before.

Quite naturally she was distraught and asked if I would pray for her. We joined hands and I fervently lifted her need to the Lord. She dried her tears and rose to leave,

As I walked her to the door, I apologized for not remembering her name or the fact that she had attended our home group before. "That's alright," she said, "I didn't remember your name either. I just knew this was the house where you could get prayer."

I closed the door, leaned against it and prayed another prayer, "Oh, Lord, I thank you that it's not about us, it's about YOU. You are already working in people's lives and are just allowing us the privilege of sharing the experience.

It Was Thursday Night!

"Counsel of a Different Kind"

The crowd was unusually small that Thursday night. No wonder, the weather was terrible, cold and stormy. We pulled our chairs closer to the fireplace as we sipped hot coffee. After worshipping in song we got into our Bible study and the doorbell rang. "It must be visitors," I said, "No-one bothers to ring the bell on Thursday nights."

As I opened the door, my jaw dropped. There stood our former next door neighbors from Leakesville, Mississippi, John and Becky Miller. We had not seen them in nearly fifteen years. "Don't ask me what we're doing here," said Becky, "Something just told us to come." They had driven a hundred miles and it was approaching 9:00 P.M. They had our address, but not a phone number.

"What are you doing?" she inquired, "Playing bridge?" I ushered them in, "Come in, come in. Actually, we're having a Bible study. Please have a seat and let me get you some hot coffee." Friends made way to pull more chairs around the cozy fire.

Don't let us stop you from your Bible study," John said, so we continued on. As was our custom, we asked about people's prayer needs. "Now I know why we're here," Becky spoke as she also began to cry. "I thought we were coming to ask Dr. Jim for some medical counsel. You see, I have been diagnosed with cancer, but this is what I really need, prayer."

They had no idea that we had regular Thursday night Bible study-prayer meetings. They came in response to an inner prompting. The Lord is so good. He kept the group small that night, an intimate group of true intercessors who were genuinely concerned about these worried and weary old friends so desperate for help. We did what the Bible says to do in James 5:14-15: "Is any sick among you? He should call for the elders of the church to pray over him and anoint him with oil in the name of the Lord. And the prayer offered in faith will make the sick person well."

We had more than one elder in the group and we always had a vial of anointing oil available for just such occasions. Becky gratefully received the prayers and anointing with oil. Relief spread over her face.

They would not stay the night, even though I insisted sincerely. They would drive the one hundred miles back home. "We got what we came for." were their parting words.

It Was Thursday Night!

"Intercession"

The worship had been exceptionally good and the crowd was large that night. A lot of people were sitting on the floor. Carolyn Lero was in her usual "wallowed out" place on the carpet, resting her back against the sofa. She was greatly endowed with the gifts of the Spirit, especially with the gifts of prophecy and exhortation. We all respected her because she was a woman of great faith and really seemed to hear from God.

We were deep into our Bible study when Carolyn suddenly jumped up and fell on her knees before Jim's wheelchair. "We've got to pray, we've got to pray right now! Tom McKenney is in danger! We have to pray NOW! She began praying in her prayer language. Others around the room joined in fervent intercession for our beloved brother in the Lord, Tom, who was on a mission trip to Belize. Some prayed in English, others in their prayer languages, but for sure, we were of one accord.

We knew little of Tom's whereabouts except that he and a companion, Greg Owen, were traveling in a very old truck hauling equipment to a ministry in Belize, via Texas and Mexico.

Later, we found out that at the very hour we were praying, the truck had broken down on an extremely dangerous stretch of mountainous road. The truck had lost all power so it had no lights as it sat in the pitch dark night. Truly a cliff-hanger story. The men were literally on the edge of a

281

steep cliff, with no guard rail protection. Furthermore, the drivers in those mountain areas were familiar with the roads and drove recklessly. At every approaching vehicle, Tom and Greg feared for their lives and had no way to signal danger to the other drivers. They attribute their survival to the prayers of our group and the protection of an all-powerful God.

It Was Thursday Night!

ACKNOWLEDGMENTS

My deepest appreciation to my two lovely daughters, Debby Levy and Dawn Nelson, for their editing and proof-reading skills on the manuscript. I couldn't have done it without you.

To my dear husband, Bill Sides, for your photography and computer skills. What invaluable help and such a patient man.

To my son, Kenny Tanner (better known to the family as 'Golden Boy'), thanks for keeping the electronics working; also for your forth-coming help with the distribution of the book.

To Mike Gillespie of Cutting Edge Design, LLC. Truly God used you in rescuing my former home, Merrywood, in Pass Christian, Mississippi; having it moved to its new location on the Scenic Drive and then restoring it beyond its former glory. May the legacy of Merrywood continue!

To the nice folks at Wyatt House Publishing in Mobile, Alabama for helping me realize my dream of sharing God's grace in our lives.

To Bill and Anna Rouse Anderson for recommending Wyatt House Publishing to me.

Thanks to all!

Wyatt House Publishing

You have a story.
We want to publish it.

Everyone has as a story to tell. It might be about something you know how to do, or what has happened in your life, or it may be a thrilling, or romantic, or intriguing, or heartwarming, or suspenseful story, starring a cast of characters that have been swimming around in your imagination.

And at Wyatt House Publishing, we can get your story onto the pages of a book just like the one you are holding in your hand. With professional interior design and a custom, professionally designed cover built just for you from the start, you can finally see your dream of being an author become reality. Then, you will see your book listed with retailers all over the world as people are able to buy your book from wherever they are and have it delivered to their home or their e-reader.

So what are you waiting for? This is your time.

visit us at
www.wyattpublishing.com

for details on how to get started becoming a published author right away.

CPSIA information can be obtained
at www.ICGtesting.com
Printed in the USA
LVOW01s1938081216
516457LV00002B/2/P